What Is Comprehension?

Comprehension is a cognitive process. It involves the capacity of the mind to understand, using logic and reasoning. For students, it should be more than a process of trying to guess the answers to formal exercises after reading text. Students need to know **how to think about and make decisions about a text before, during, and after reading it**.

Teaching Comprehension

Comprehension skills can and should be developed by teaching students strategies that are appropriate to a particular comprehension skill and then providing opportunities for them to discuss and practice applying those strategies to the texts they read. These strategies can be a series of clearly defined steps to follow.

Students need to understand that it is the **process**—not the product—that is more important. In other words, they need to understand how it is done before they are required to demonstrate that they can do it.

Higher-order comprehension skills are within the capacity of young students, but care needs to be taken to ensure that the level and language of the text is appropriately assigned.

The text can be read to the students. When introducing comprehension strategies to students, the emphasis should be on the discussion, and the comprehension activities should be completed orally before moving on to supported and then independent practice and application. The lessons in this book are scaffolded to accommodate this process.

Note: Some students may not be able to complete the activities independently. For those students, additional support should be provided as they work through the activities within each unit.

Before students start the activities in this book, discuss the concepts of paragraphs and stanzas. Note that the paragraphs in each reading passage or stanza have been numbered for easy reference as students complete activities.

The terms *skills* and *strategies* are sometimes confused. The following explanation provides some clarification of how the two terms are used in this book.

Skills relate to competent performance and come from knowledge, practice, and aptitude.

Strategies involve planning and tactics.

In other words, we can teach *strategies* that will help students acquire specific comprehension *skills*.

Twelve comprehension skills are introduced in this book. Information about these skills and how the units and lessons are designed to explore them are provided on pages 4 – 6.

Metacognitive Strategies

Metacognitive strategies which involve teaching students how to think are used in developing the twelve comprehension skills in this book. Metacognitive strategies are the chief components for each skill. As this process is modeled, students are encouraged to elaborate on the explanations provided on each "Learning Page." The activities on these pages allow students to talk about the different thought processes they would use in answering each question.

Students will require different levels of support before they are able to work independently to comprehend, make decisions about text, and choose the best answer in multiple-choice questions. This support is provided within each unit lesson by including guided practice, modeled practice using the metacognitive processes, and assisted practice using hints and clues.

Comprehension Strategies

The exercises in this book have been written—not to test—but to stimulate and challenge students and to help them develop their thinking processes through modeled metacognitive strategies, discussion, and guided and independent practice. There are no trick questions, but many require and encourage students to use logic and reasoning.

Particularly in the higher-order comprehension skills, there may be more than one acceptable answer. The reader's prior knowledge and experience will influence some of his or her decisions about the text. Teachers may choose to accept an answer if a student can justify and explain his or her choice. Therefore, some of the answers provided should not be considered prescriptive but more of a guide and a basis for discussion.

Some students with excellent cognitive processing skills, who have a particular aptitude for and acquire an interest in reading, tend to develop advanced reading comprehension skills independently. However, for the majority of students, the strategies they need to develop and demonstrate comprehension need to be made explicit and carefully guided, not just tested, which is the rationale behind this series of books.

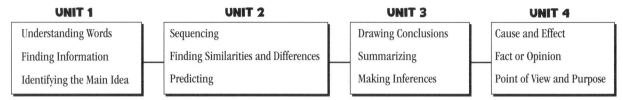
The following twelve comprehension skills are included in this book. Strategies for improving these skills are provided through sets of lessons for each of the skills. These twelve skills have been divided into four units, each with teachers' notes and answer keys, three different comprehension skills, and three student assessment tests.

UNIT 1	UNIT 2	UNIT 3	UNIT 4
Understanding Words	Sequencing	Drawing Conclusions	Cause and Effect
Finding Information	Finding Similarities and Differences	Summarizing	Fact or Opinion
Identifying the Main Idea	Predicting	Making Inferences	Point of View and Purpose

Each skill listed above has a six-page lesson to help students build stronger comprehension skills in that area by using specific strategies.

- Text 1 (first reading text page for use with practice pages)
- Learning Page (learning about the skill with teacher modeling)
- Practice Page (student practice with teacher assistance)
- On Your Own (independent student activity)
- Text 2 (second reading text page for use with practice page)
- Try It Out (independent student activity with one clue)

Text Types

A test at the end of each unit assesses the three skills taught in the unit. The assessment section includes:

- Assessment Text (reading text used for all three assessments)
- Assessment test for the first skill in the unit
- Assessment test for the second skill in the unit
- Assessment test for the third skill in the unit

Included in this book is a CD containing reproducible, PDF-formatted files for all activity pages, as well as Common Core State Standards. The PDF files are ideal for group instruction using interactive whiteboards.

In addition to applying comprehension strategies to better understand content, students will experience reading and interpreting a variety of text types:

- Reports
- Narratives
- Expositions
- Recounts
- Procedures
- Explanations

Teacher and Student Pages

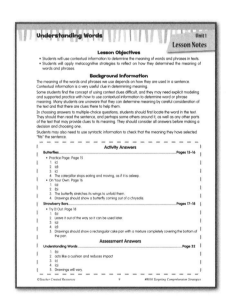

Lesson Notes

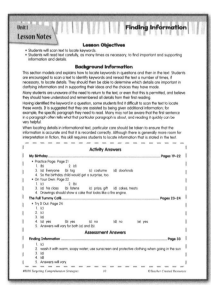

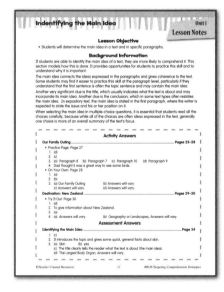

Each of the four units contains lessons that address three specific comprehension skills. Every Lesson Notes page includes:

- Lesson objective indicators state expected outcomes.

- Background information about the skill and teaching strategies.

- An answer key for student pages and assessment pages. (*Note:* Answers may vary, particularly with higher-order comprehension skills. Teachers may choose to accept alternative answers if students are able to justify their responses.)

Editors

Mary S. Jones, M.A.

Cristina Krysinski, M. Ed.

Editor in Chief

Karen J. Goldfluss, M.S. Ed.

Creative Director

Sarah M. Smith

Cover Artist

Diem Pascarella

Art Coordinator

Renée McElwee

Imaging

Ariyanna Simien

Publisher

Mary D. Smith, M.S. Ed.

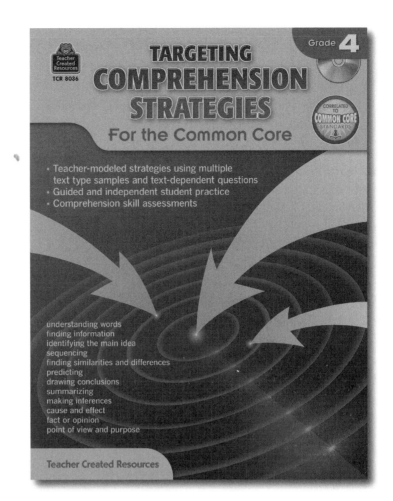

The lessons and activities in each unit have been correlated to Common Core State Standards for English Language Arts. Correlations charts are provided on pages 7 and 8 and can also be found at *http://www.teachercreated.com/standards*.

Teacher Created Resources

6421 Industry Way

Westminster, CA 92683

www.teachercreated.com

ISBN: 978-1-4206-8036-2

© 2014 Teacher Created Resources

Made in U.S.A.

Table of Contents

Helpful Hints

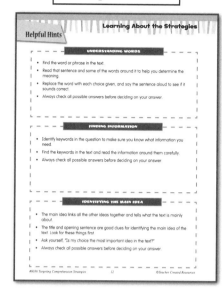

- All three comprehension skills for the unit are identified. These serve as reminders for students as they complete the activities.

- Helpful hints are provided for each skill in bullet-point form.

Text 1

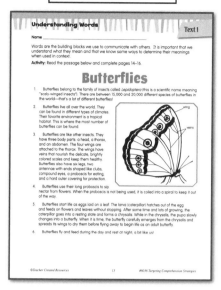

- The skill is identified and defined.

- The text is presented to students using oral, silent, partner, or read-aloud methods. Choose a technique or approach most suitable to your classroom needs.

Learning Page

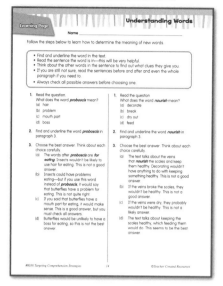

- This is a teacher-student interaction page.

- Steps and strategies are outlined, discussed, and referenced using the text page.

- Multiple-choice questions are presented, and metacognitive processes for choosing the best answer are described.

Practice Page

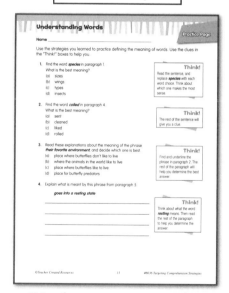

- Using the text page content, students practice strategies to complete the questions. The teacher provides guidance as needed.

- Some multiple-choice questions and others requiring explanations are presented with prompts or clues to assist students.

On Your Own

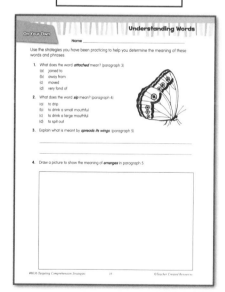

- This page is completed independently.

- At least one multiple-choice question and others requiring explanations are presented for students to complete.

Text 2

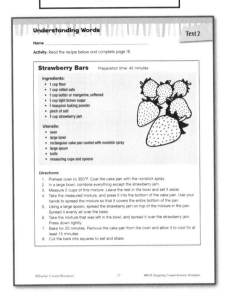

- As with the first text page for the lesson, the skill is identified.

- Presentation of the text is decided by the teacher.

Try It Out

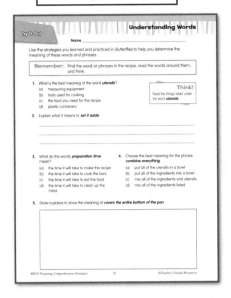

- This page can be completed independently by the student.

- Multiple-choice questions and some requiring explanation are included.

Assessment Text

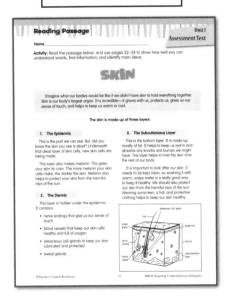

- The three skills to be tested are identified.

- The assessment text is presented.

Unit Assessments

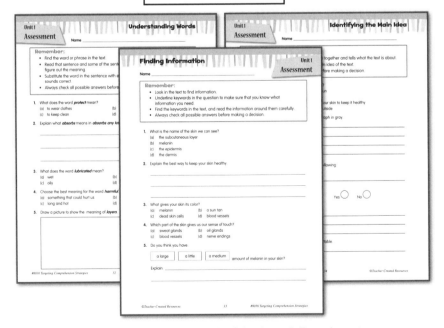

- An assessment page is provided for each of the three skills in the unit.

- The comprehension skill to be tested is identified, and students apply their knowledge and strategies to complete each page, using the content of the Assessment Text page.

- Multiple-choice questions and others requiring more explanation are presented.

Common Core State Standards Correlations

Each lesson meets one or more of the following Common Core State Standards © Copyright 2010. National Governors Association Center for Best Practices and Council of Chief State School Officers. All rights reserved. For more information about the Common Core State Standards, go to *http://www.corestandards.org/* or *http://www.teachercreated.com/standards*.

READING: LITERATURE STANDARDS	Pages
Key Ideas and Details	
ELA.RL.4.1: Refer to details and examples in a text when explaining what the text says explicitly and when drawing inferences from the text.	19-22, 25-28 ,39-42 ,51-54, 55-56, 57-60, 69-70, 75-76, 77-80, 81-82, 83-86,101-102,109-112
ELA.RL.4.2: Determine a theme of a story, drama, or poem from details in the text; summarize the text.	19-22, 25-28, 39-42, 51-54, 55-56, 57-60, 69-70, 75-76, 77-80, 81-82, 83-86, 101-102, 107-108, 109-112
ELA.RL.4.3: Describe in depth a character, setting, or event in a story or drama, drawing on specific details in the text (e.g., a character's thoughts, words, or actions).	19-22, 39-42, 51-54, 55-56, 57-60, 77-80, 81-82, 109-112
Craft and Structure	
ELA.RL.4.4: Determine the meaning of words and phrases as they are used in a text, including those that allude to significant characters found in mythology (e.g., Herculean).	19-22, 25-28, 39-42, 51-54,55-56, 57-60, 69-70, 75-76, 77-80, 81-82, 83-86,101-102, 107-108, 109-112
Range of Reading and Complexity of Text	
ELA.RL.4.10: By the end of the year, read and comprehend literature, including stories, dramas, and poetry, in the grades 4–5 text complexity band proficiently, with scaffolding as needed at the high end of the range.	All literature/fiction passages allow students to read and comprehend literature in the grades 4-5 text complexity band proficiently.

READING: INFORMATIONAL TEXT STANDARDS	Pages
Key Ideas and Details	
ELA.RI.4.1: Refer to details and examples in a text when explaining what the text says explicitly and when drawing inferences from the text.	13-16, 17-18, 23-24, 29-30, 31-34, 43-44, 45-48, 49-50, 65-68, 71-74, 91-94, 95-96, 97-100, 103-106

READING: INFORMATIONAL TEXT STANDARDS *(cont.)*	Pages
Key Ideas and Details	
ELA.RI.4.2: Determine the main idea of a text and explain how it is supported by key details; summarize the text.	13-16, 29-30, 31-34, 43-44, 65-68, 71-74, 91-94, 97-100, 103-106
ELA.RI.4.3: Explain events, procedures, ideas, or concepts in a historical, scientific, or technical text, including what happened and why, based on specific information in the text.	13-16, 17-18, 29-30, 31-34, 43-44, 45-48, 65-68, 71-74, 95-96
Craft and Structure	
ELA.RI.4.4: Determine the meaning of general academic and domain-specific words or phrases in a text relevant to a grade 4 topic or subject area.	13-16, 17-18, 23-24, 29-30, 31-34, 43-44, 45-48, 49-50, 65-68, 71-74, 91-94, 95-96, 97-100, 103-106
ELA.RI.4.5: Describe the overall structure (e.g., chronology, comparison, cause/effect, problem/solution) of events, ideas, concepts, or information in a text or part of a text.	43-44, 45-48, 49-50, 91-94, 95-96, 97-100, 103-106
Integration of Knowledge and Ideas	
ELA.RI.4.7: Interpret information presented visually, orally, or quantitatively (e.g., in charts, graphs, diagrams, time lines, animations, or interactive elements on Web pages) and explain how the information contributes to an understanding of the text in which it appears.	13-16, 17-18, 23-24, 29-30, 31-34, 43-44, 45-48, 49-50, 71-74, 95-96
ELA.RI.4.8: Explain how an author uses reasons and evidence to support particular points in a text.	49-50, 65-68, 71-74, 91-94, 97-100, 103-106
Range of Reading and Level of Text Complexity	
Standard 10: RI.4.10 By the end of year, read and comprehend informational texts, including history/social studies, science, and technical texts, in the grades 4–5 text complexity band proficiently, with scaffolding as needed at the high end of the range.	All nonfiction passages allow students to read and comprehend informational texts in the grades 4-5 text complexity band.

Lesson Objectives

- Students will use contextual information to determine the meaning of words and phrases in texts.
- Students will apply metacognitive strategies to reflect on how they determined the meaning of words and phrases.

Background Information

The meaning of the words and phrases we use depends on how they are used in a sentence. Contextual information is a very useful clue in determining meaning.

Some students find the concept of using context clues difficult, and they may need explicit modeling and supported practice with how to use contextual information to determine word or phrase meaning. Many students are unaware that they can determine meaning by careful consideration of the text and that there are clues there to help them.

In choosing answers to multiple-choice questions, students should first locate the word in the text. They should then read the sentence, and perhaps some others around it, as well as any other parts of the text that may provide clues to its meaning. They should consider all answers before making a decision and choosing one.

Students may also need to use syntactic information to check that the meaning they have selected "fits" the sentence.

Activity Answers

Butterflies..**Pages 13–16**

- Practice Page: Page 15
  1. (c)
  2. (d)
  3. (c)
  4. The caterpillar stops eating and moving, as if it is asleep.
- On Your Own: Page 16
  1. (a)
  2. (b)
  3. The butterfly stretches its wings to unfold them.
  4. Drawings should show a butterfly coming out of a chrysalis.

Strawberry Bars..**Pages 17–18**

- Try It Out: Page 18
  1. (b)
  2. Leave it out of the way so it can be used later.
  3. (a)
  4. (d)
  5. Drawings should show a rectangular cake pan with a mixture completely covering the bottom of the pan.

Assessment Answers

Understanding Words ....**Page 32**

1. (b)
2. acts like a cushion and reduces impact
3. (c)
4. (a)
5. Drawings will vary.

Lesson Objectives

- Students will scan text to locate keywords.
- Students will read text carefully, as many times as necessary, to find important and supporting information and details.

Background Information

This section models and explains how to locate keywords in questions and then in the text. Students are encouraged to scan a text to identify keywords and reread the text a number of times, if necessary, to locate details. They should then be able to determine which details are important in clarifying information and in supporting their ideas and the choices they have made.

Many students are unaware of the need to return to the text, or even that this is permitted, and believe they should have understood and remembered all details from their first reading.

Having identified the keyword in a question, some students find it difficult to scan the text to locate these words. It is suggested that they are assisted by being given additional information; for example, the specific paragraph they need to read. Many may not be aware that the first sentence in a paragraph often tells what that particular paragraph is about, and reading it quickly can be very helpful.

When locating details in informational text, particular care should be taken to ensure that the information is accurate and that it is recorded correctly. Although there is generally more room for interpretation in fiction, this skill requires students to locate information that is stated in the text.

Activity Answers

My Birthday ....**Pages 19–22**

- Practice Page: Page 21
  1. (b)   2. (d)
  3. (a) Everyone   (b) tag   (c) costume   (d) doorknob
  4. So the birthday child would get a surprise, too.
- On Your Own: Page 22
  1. (c)   2. (b)
  3. (a) his class   (b) listens   (c) prize; gift   (d) cakes; treats
  4. Drawings should show a cake that looks like a fire engine.

The Full Tummy Café ....**Pages 23–24**

- Try It Out: Page 24
  1. (c)
  2. (c)
  3. (a)
  4. (a) yes   (b) yes   (c) no   (d) no   (e) yes
  5. Answers will vary for both (a) and (b).

Assessment Answers

Finding Information ....**Page 33**

  1. (c)
  2. wash it with warm, soapy water; use sunscreen and protective clothing when going in the sun
  3. (a)
  4. (d)
  5. Answers will vary.

Indentifying the Main Idea

Lesson Objective

- Students will determine the main idea in a text and in specific paragraphs.

Background Information

If students are able to identify the main idea of a text, they are more likely to comprehend it. This section models how this is done. It provides opportunities for students to practice this skill and to understand why it is important.

The main idea connects the ideas expressed in the paragraphs and gives coherence to the text. Some students may find it easier to practice this skill at the paragraph level, particularly if they understand that the first sentence is often the topic sentence and may contain the main idea.

Another very significant clue is the title, which usually indicates what the text is about and may incorporate its main idea. Another clue is the conclusion, which in some text types often restates the main idea. In expository text, the main idea is stated in the first paragraph, where the writer is expected to state the issue and his or her position on it.

When selecting the main idea in multiple-choice questions, it is essential that students read all the choices carefully, because while all of the choices are often ideas expressed in the text, generally one choice is more of an overall summary of the text's focus.

Activity Answers

Our Family Outing .... **Pages 25–28**

- Practice Page: Page 27
  1. (d)
  2. (c)
  3. (a) Paragraph 8   (b) Paragraph 7   (c) Paragraph 10   (d) Paragraph 9
  4. Dad thought it was a great way to see some birds.
- On Your Own: Page 28
  1. (a)
  2. (b)
  3. (a) Our Family Outing   (b) Answers will vary.
     (c) Answers will vary.   (d) Answers will vary.

Destination: New Zealand .... **Pages 29–30**

- Try It Out: Page 30
  1. (d)
  2. To give information about New Zealand.
  3. (a)
  4. (a) Answers will vary.   (b) Geography or Landscapes; Answers will vary.

Assessment Answers

Identifying the Main Idea .... **Page 34**

1. (c)
2. It introduces the topic and gives some quick, general facts about skin.
3. (a) Skin   (b) yes
   (c) The title clearly tells the reader what the text is about (the main idea).
   (d) The Largest Body Organ; Answers will vary.

Helpful Hints

UNDERSTANDING WORDS

- Find the word or phrase in the text.
- Read that sentence and some of the words around it to help you determine the meaning.
- Replace the word with each choice given, and say the sentence aloud to see if it sounds correct.
- Always check all possible answers before deciding on your answer.

FINDING INFORMATION

- Identify keywords in the question to make sure you know what information you need.
- Find the keywords in the text and read the information around them carefully.
- Always check all possible answers before deciding on your answer.

IDENTIFYING THE MAIN IDEA

- The main idea links all the other ideas together and tells what the text is mainly about.
- The title and opening sentence are good clues for identifying the main idea of the text. Look for these things first.
- Ask yourself, "Is my choice the most important idea in the text?"
- Always check all possible answers before deciding on your answer.

Name _____

Words are the building blocks we use to communicate with others. It is important that we understand what they mean and that we know some ways to determine their meanings when used in context.

Activity: Read the passage below and complete pages 14–16.

Butterflies

1. Butterflies belong to the family of insects called *Lepidoptera* (this is a scientific name meaning "scaly-winged insects"). There are between 15,000 and 20,000 different species of butterflies in the world—that's a lot of different butterflies!

2. Butterflies live all over the world. They can be found in different types of climates. Their favorite environment is a tropical habitat. This is where the most number of butterflies can be found.

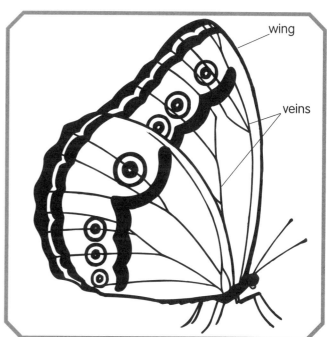

3. Butterflies are like other insects. They have three body parts: a head, a thorax, and an abdomen. The four wings are attached to the thorax. The wings have veins that nourish the delicate, brightly colored scales and keep them healthy. Butterflies also have six legs, two antennae with ends shaped like clubs, compound eyes, a proboscis for eating, and a hard outer covering for protection.

4. Butterflies use their long proboscis to sip nectar from flowers. When the proboscis is not being used, it is coiled into a spiral to keep it out of the way.

5. Butterflies start life as eggs laid on a leaf. The larva (caterpillar) hatches out of the egg and feeds on flowers and leaves without stopping. After some time and lots of growing, the caterpillar goes into a resting state and forms a chrysalis. While in the chrysalis, the pupa slowly changes into a butterfly. When it is time, the butterfly carefully emerges from the chrysalis and spreads its wings to dry them before flying away to begin life as an adult butterfly.

6. Butterflies fly and feed during the day and rest at night; a bit like us!

Learning Page

Name _____

Follow the steps below to learn how to determine the meaning of new words.

- Find and underline the word in the text.
- Read the sentence the word is in—this will be very helpful.
- Think about the other words in the sentence to find out what clues they give you.
- If you are still not sure, read the sentences before and after and even the whole paragraph if you need to.
- Always check all possible answers before choosing one.

1. Read the question.
   What does the word *proboscis* mean?
   (a) hair
   (b) problem
   (c) mouth part
   (d) boss

2. Find and underline the word *proboscis* in paragraph 3.

3. Choose the best answer. Think about each choice carefully.
   (a) The words after *proboscis* are *for eating*. Insects wouldn't be likely to use hair for eating. This is not a good answer.
   (b) Insects could have problems eating—but if you use this word instead of *proboscis*, it would say that butterflies have a problem for eating. This is not quite right.
   (c) If you said that butterflies have a mouth part for eating, it would make sense. This is a good answer, but you must check all answers.
   (d) Butterflies would be unlikely to have a boss for eating, so this is not the best answer.

1. Read the question
   What does the word *nourish* mean?
   (a) decorate
   (b) break
   (c) dry out
   (d) feed

2. Find and underline the word *nourish* in paragraph 3.

3. Choose the best answer. Think about each choice carefully.
   (a) The text talks about the veins that *nourish* the scales and keep them healthy. Decorating wouldn't have anything to do with keeping something healthy. This is not a good answer.
   (b) If the veins broke the scales, they wouldn't be healthy. This is not a good answer.
   (c) If the veins were dry, they probably wouldn't be healthy. This is not a likely answer.
   (d) The text talks about keeping the scales healthy, which feeding them would do. This seems to be the best answer.

Understanding Words

Name _____

Use the strategies you learned to practice defining the meaning of words. Use the clues in the "Think!" boxes to help you.

1. Find the word **species** in paragraph 1.
   What is the best meaning?
   (a)   sizes
   (b)   wings
   (c)   types
   (d)   insects

   > **Think!**
   > Read the sentence, and replace **species** with each word choice. Think about which one makes the most sense.

2. Find the word **coiled** in paragraph 4.
   What is the best meaning?
   (a)   sent
   (b)   cleaned
   (c)   liked
   (d)   rolled

   > **Think!**
   > The rest of the sentence will give you a clue.

3. Read these explanations about the meaning of the phrase **their favorite environment**, and decide which one is best.
   (a)   place where butterflies don't like to live
   (b)   where the animals in the world like to live
   (c)   place where butterflies like to live
   (d)   place for butterfly predators

   > **Think!**
   > Find and underline the phrase in paragraph 2. The rest of the paragraph will help you determine the best answer.

4. Explain what is meant by this phrase from paragraph 5:

   goes into a resting state

   _____

   _____

   _____

   _____

   > **Think!**
   > Think about what the word **resting** means. Then read the rest of the paragraph to help you determine the answer.

Name _____

Use the strategies you have been practicing to help you determine the meaning of these words and phrases.

1. What does the word *attached* mean? (paragraph 3)

    (a) joined to

    (b) away from

    (c) moved

    (d) very fond of

2. What does the word *sip* mean? (paragraph 4)

    (a) to drip

    (b) to drink a small mouthful

    (c) to drink a large mouthful

    (d) to spit out

3. Explain what is meant by *spreads its wings*. (paragraph 5)

    _____

    _____

4. Draw a picture to show the meaning of *emerges* in paragraph 5.

Understanding Words

Name _____

Activity: Read the recipe below and complete page 18.

Strawberry Bars   *Preparation time: 45 minutes*

Ingredients:

- 1 cup flour
- 1 cup rolled oats
- $\frac{1}{2}$ cup butter or margarine, softened
- $\frac{1}{3}$ cup light brown sugar
- $\frac{1}{4}$ teaspoon baking powder
- pinch of salt
- $\frac{3}{4}$ cup strawberry jam

Utensils:

- oven
- large bowl
- rectangular cake pan coated with nonstick spray
- large spoon
- knife
- measuring cups and spoons

Directions:

1. Preheat oven to 350°F. Coat the cake pan with the nonstick spray.
2. In a large bowl, combine everything except the strawberry jam.
3. Measure 2 cups of this mixture. Leave the rest in the bowl and set it aside.
4. Take the measured mixture, and press it into the bottom of the cake pan. Use your hands to spread the mixture so that it covers the entire bottom of the pan.
5. Using a large spoon, spread the strawberry jam on top of the mixture in the pan. Spread it evenly all over the base.
6. Take the mixture that was left in the bowl, and spread it over the strawberry jam. Press down lightly.
7. Bake for 25 minutes. Remove the cake pan from the oven and allow it to cool for at least 15 minutes.
8. Cut the bars into squares to eat and share.

out

Name _____

Use the strategies you learned and practiced in *Butterflies* to help you determine the meaning of these words and phrases.

> **Remember:** Find the word or phrases in the recipe, read the words around them, and think.

1. What is the best meaning of the word ***utensils***?

    (a) measuring equipment

    (b) tools used for cooking

    (c) the food you need for the recipe

    (d) plastic containers

> **Think!**
> Read the things listed under the word ***utensils***.

2. Explain what it means to ***set it aside***.

    _____

    _____

    _____

3. What do the words ***preparation time*** mean?

    (a) the time it will take to make the recipe

    (b) the time it will take to cook the bars

    (c) the time it will take to eat the food

    (d) the time it will take to clean up the mess

4. Choose the best meaning for the phrase ***combine everything***.

    (a) put all of the utensils in a bowl

    (b) put all of the ingredients into a bowl

    (c) mix all of the ingredients and utensils

    (d) mix all of the ingredients listed

5. Draw a picture to show the meaning of ***covers the entire bottom of the pan***.

Name _____

When you read, you can usually remember some of the information you have read. If you are asked about details, you should refer back to the text to locate the information and check that it is correct. Remember, the answer you are looking for is there in the text—you just need to find it.

Activity: Read the story below and complete pages 20–22.

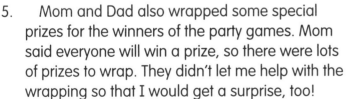

My Birthday

1. I'm so excited! It's only one day until my birthday!

2. Mom and I made my birthday invitations on the computer. We wanted to make them unique, so we used a photograph of an old fire engine to decorate them. I typed the party details and included each person's name. I took the invitations to school and delivered them to the kids in my class two weeks ago. Everyone is coming to my party.

3. Mom has been busy baking cakes and special treats for my party. She is making me a birthday cake decorated as a fire engine. Mom lets me help in the kitchen, provided I wash my hands, wear an apron, and listen carefully to her instructions—I love helping Mom cook!

4. I also helped Dad make party bags to give to my guests at the end of the party. It's a special "thank you" gift for coming. We put lots of treats inside and tied a name tag on each one. I think we did a great job! I hope my friends like their thank-you bags.

5. Mom and Dad also wrapped some special prizes for the winners of the party games. Mom said everyone will win a prize, so there were lots of prizes to wrap. They didn't let me help with the wrapping so that I would get a surprise, too!

6. Dad carefully ironed my birthday costume— a firefighter's uniform! Mom hung it up on my doorknob ready for me to wear. I think I am going to be too excited to sleep tonight. I guess the sooner I fall asleep, the sooner I will wake up—then it will be my birthday! I can't wait until tomorrow.

Name _____

Follow the steps below to learn how to find information in text.

> - Read the question very carefully. Keywords in the question will tell you what information and details you need to find. Underline them.
> - Think about an answer, but you will need to refer back to the text to check that you are correct.
> - Find the keywords in the text and carefully read the information around them.
> - Check all the possible answers before making a decision.

1. Read the question.
   How were the invitations unique?

   (a) They were made on the computer.
   (b) The boy typed the party details on them.
   (c) They were delivered to the kids at school.
   (d) A photograph of an old fire engine was used to decorate them.

2. Underline the keyword *unique* in the question and in the text. Read the information around it.

3. Choose the best answer. Think about each choice carefully.

   (a) The invitations were made on the computer, but so are lots of invitations. That wouldn't make them unique. This is not the best answer.
   (b) Typing the party details wouldn't make them unique. This is not a good answer.
   (c) Delivering invitations is a nice way to hand them out, but it doesn't make them unique. This answer is not a good choice.
   (d) The text says, "we wanted to make them *unique*, so we used a photograph of an old fire engine to decorate them." This is the best answer.

1. Read the question.
   Why were party bags made for the party?

   (a) It gave Mom something to do with her son.
   (b) They were prizes for the party games.
   (c) They were gifts for the guests as a "thank you" at the end of the party.
   (d) Mom liked making treats.

2. The keywords are *party bags*. Underline them and read the information.

3. Choose the best answer. Think about each choice carefully.

   (a) Dad and the boy made the party bags. This isn't a good answer.
   (b) Mom and Dad wrapped the prizes. This answer is not a good choice.
   (c) The text says, "it's a special 'thank you' gift." This seems like the right answer.
   (d) Mom cooked the treats for the party, not the party bags. This can't be right.

Finding Information

Name _____

Use the strategies you learned to practice finding information. Use the clues in the "Think!" boxes to help you.

1. What was the theme of the party?
    (a)   everybody helping
    (b)   firefighting
    (c)   being excited
    (d)   party prizes and gifts for everyone

> **Think!**
> The theme is the main idea of the party. It is mentioned three times in the text.

2. When did the boy give out his invitations?
    (a)   two days ago
    (b)   last week
    (c)   three weeks ago
    (d)   two weeks ago

> **Think!**
> Read paragraph 2 to find the answer.

3. Find words from the text to complete these sentences.

    (a)   _____ who was invited is coming to the party.

    (b)   A name _____ was tied onto each party bag.

> **Think!**
> Find keywords in each sentence and match keywords in the text.

    (c)   The boy's birthday _____ was a firefighter's uniform.

    (d)   The uniform was hung on the _____, ready to wear.

4. Explain why Mom and Dad wanted to wrap the prizes themselves.

    _____

    _____

    _____

    _____

> **Think!**
> Read the paragraph that talks about the prizes carefully.

On Your Own

Name _____

Use the strategies you have been practicing to help you find the information in the text.

1. Why was the boy excited?
   - (a) because he liked fire engines
   - (b) because he liked to help Mom in the kitchen
   - (c) because it was only one more day until his birthday
   - (d) because he wanted to dress up as a firefighter

2. How did Dad help get ready for the party?
   - (a) He typed the text on the invitations.
   - (b) He made the party bags, wrapped the prizes, and ironed the clothes.
   - (c) He delivered the invitations.
   - (d) He made the party bags and baked the cake.

3. Find words from the text to complete these sentences.

   (a) The kids from _____ were invited to the party.

   (b) The boy can help Mom in the kitchen provided he

   _____ carefully to instructions.

   (c) All the guests will take home a _____ and a

   thank-you _____.

   (d) Mom baked _____ and special

   _____ for the birthday party.

4. Draw a picture to show what the birthday cake looked like.

Name _____

Activity: Read the menu below and complete page 24.

The Full Tummy Café

BREAKFAST   6 a.m. – 10 a.m.

Served with milk
Oatmeal $4.50
Mini muffins $4.00
Cold cereal $3.00

Fresh fruit
Mixed bowl of fresh fruit $4.50
Mixed bowl of fresh fruit with yogurt ... $5.50

Pancake stack with . . .
Maple syrup $4.50
Lemon and sugar.............................. $4.50
Mixed fresh berries $6.00
Ice cream...................................... $5.50

Eggs on toast
Fried.. $4.00
Scrambled..................................... $4.00
Poached....................................... $4.00
Sunny side up................................ $3.50
Big Breakfast—bacon, egg, sausage,
   tomato, mushrooms,
   and toast.................................... $9.50

BEVERAGES   all day

Hot
Cappuccino................................... $2.50
Caffé latte.................................... $2.50
Tea.. $1.50
Hot chocolate................................ $3.00

Juices and Milk
Orange.. $2.00
Apple $2.00
Pineapple..................................... $2.00
Cranberry..................................... $2.00
Milk $2.00

Other drinks
Lemonade..................................... $2.50
Cola $2.50
Root beer..................................... $2.50

LUNCH/DINNER   10 a.m. – 10 p.m.

Sandwiches and rolls (wheat or white)
Chicken....................................... $4.00
Chicken and salad $5.50
Ham... $3.00
Ham and salad $4.50
Tuna... $3.00
Tuna and salad $4.50
Egg $3.50
Egg and salad................................ $5.00

(salad includes lettuce, tomato, carrot, and cucumber)

Hot foods
Hamburger and fries......................... $5.50
Cheeseburger and fries $6.00
Fish and chips $6.00
Spaghetti and meatballs $7.50
Beef curry with rice.......................... $9.00
Vegetable stir-fry with noodles.............. $9.00
Fried rice...................................... $7.00
Pork and vegetable kebabs $7.00
Vegetarian pizza $7.50
Soup of the day with crispy bread......... $5.50

Salads
Caesar $8.50
Greek.. $7.50
Spinach, bacon, and pine nut $7.50
Chicken and snow pea $7.50
Pasta and prawn............................. $8.50

DESSERTS   all day

Hot
Apple pie with ice cream..................... $4.50
Bread and butter pudding $4.50
Strawberry crumble and cream............ $5.00

Cold
Cheesecake................................... $4.50
Lemon meringue pie......................... $4.50
Fruit salad and ice cream $5.50
Chocolate cake $5.50

Name _____

Use the strategies you learned and practiced in *My Birthday* to help you find information.

Remember:
- Find the keywords in the questions and in the text.
- Check all answers before you make a decision.

1. What are beverages?
   - (a) hot drinks
   - (b) cold drinks
   - (c) drinks
   - (d) ingredients for drinks

Think!
Find the items in the list written below the word.

2. The open hours of the café are:
   - (a) 6 a.m. – 10 a.m.
   - (b) 10 a.m. – 10 p.m.
   - (c) 6 a.m. – 10 p.m.
   - (d) 10 p.m. – 6 a.m.

3. How much will my breakfast cost if I have pancakes with mixed fresh berries and pineapple juice?
   - (a) $8.00
   - (b) $6.00
   - (c) $4.00
   - (d) $2.00

4. Read each sentence. Choose **Yes** or **No**.

   (a) Fried rice costs more than soup.   Yes ◯   No ◯

   (b) Tuna sandwiches cost less than chicken sandwiches.   Yes ◯   No ◯

   (c) Hot chocolate and apple juice cost the same.   Yes ◯   No ◯

   (d) Fried eggs cost more than poached eggs.   Yes ◯   No ◯

   (e) Chocolate cake costs more than cheesecake.   Yes ◯   No ◯

5. Use the menu to make your selections.

   (a) What would you like to eat for lunch from this menu?

   _____

   (b) How much would it cost?

   _____

Name _____

If you know the main idea of a text, you will have a much better chance of understanding what the content is about.

Activity: Read the story below and complete pages 26–28.

Our Family Outing

1. "Okay, it's a warm and sunny day, so let's go on a picnic!" called Mom. We came running from different parts of the house, cheering loudly.

2. We loved going on picnics. We all had our jobs to do to prepare for the picnic. Georgia found the picnic blanket and put it next to the car. It was my job to get out the picnic basket and make sure the plates, cups, and cutlery were all there. I also made sure we had napkins to wipe our hands. Dad got our picnic toys and packed them in the car, while Mom made the sandwiches and fruit salad. We were ready to go!

3. We put on sunscreen and hats and piled into the car. We always sing happy songs on our way to a picnic—and today was no different. Finally, we arrived at our destination. We had never been to this place before, so there was a lot to explore.

4. "Let's go for a walk to check out the area," suggested Dad.

5. "Can I bring my binoculars?" I asked.

6. "Sure, Josh, what a great idea! We might see some birds," Dad replied.

7. We both like to spot different birds, and we often have a competition. I usually win, but I have a feeling Dad lets me! We had a great time bird-spotting. There were so many trees in the park; it was a haven for birds.

8. We stopped for lunch, which was delicious. Mom always makes the best sandwiches.

9. After lunch, Georgia and I played with our air rockets. We loved shooting them high into the air. We had competitions to see who could get the rocket to fly higher. It was so much fun!

10. "Okay guys, time to pack up and go home!" called Mom.

11. Packing up at the end of the picnic always takes us ages because we never want to go home—and today was no different!

Name _____

Follow the steps below to learn how to identify the main idea and why it is important.

- There are many ideas in a text, but only one idea is the link that joins the other ideas together—this is the main idea.
- Read the text, and then ask yourself, "What is it mainly about?" (The title is a useful clue to the main idea because a good title often tells the reader what the text is about.)
- Always check all the possible answers before making a decision.

1. Read what you need to find out.

   The main idea of *Our Family Outing* is:
   (a) how to organize a picnic.
   (b) a family arguing about where to go for a family outing.
   (c) looking for birds as a family.
   (d) a family spending the day together on a picnic.

2. Choose the best answer. Think about each choice carefully.
   (a) The second paragraph talks about getting ready for a picnic, but that isn't what the whole story is about. This isn't a good answer.
   (b) The family didn't argue in the story. This wouldn't be a good answer.
   (c) The boy and his dad do look for birds, but that isn't what the whole story is about. This wouldn't be the best answer.
   (d) The story talks about the different things the family does when getting ready for a picnic and what they do on the picnic. This is the best answer.

1. Read what you need to find out.

   The main idea of paragraph 2 is:
   (a) Mom preparing the food.
   (b) Dad getting the toys and packing the car.
   (c) getting organized for the picnic.
   (d) Georgia finding the picnic blanket.

2. Choose the best answer. Think about each choice carefully.
   (a) Mom does prepare the food, but that isn't all that happens. This is not the best answer.
   (b) Dad does get the toys and pack the car, but he is not the only one who helps to get ready for the picnic. This is probably not the right answer.
   (c) The paragraph talks about what each person does to help get ready for the picnic. This would be a good choice.
   (d) Georgia helps to get ready for the picnic, but everyone does his or her part to help. This wouldn't be the best answer.

Identifying the Main Idea

Name _____

Use the strategies you learned to practice identifying the main idea. Use the clues in the "Think!" boxes to help you.

1. What is the main idea of paragraphs 4, 5, and 6?
   (a) going on a hike
   (b) what binoculars are used for
   (c) there were lots of trees at the park
   (d) exploring the park and looking for birds

> **Think!**
> What are all the ideas in the paragraphs about?

2. What is the main idea of the last paragraph?
   (a) the amount of time it takes to get ready
   (b) the car journey
   (c) packing up to go home at the end of the day
   (d) being happy to go home at the end of the day

> **Think!**
> Think about all of the ideas in this paragraph.

3. Read the sentences below that tell the main idea for different paragraphs. Choose the paragraph number that matches each main idea.

> **Think!**
> Read paragraphs 7, 8, 9, and 10, and think what each is mainly about.

   (a) They ate Mom's delicious sandwiches for lunch.   7   8   9   10

   (b) Dad and Josh had a great time bird-spotting.   7   8   9   10

   (c) Mom said it was time to go.   7   8   9   10

   (d) Josh and Georgia had fun shooting their air rockets.   7   8   9   10

4. Explain what paragraph 6 is about.

   _____

   _____

   _____

   _____

> **Think!**
> Think about the main idea and how the writer feels about it.

On Your Own

Name _____

Use the strategies you have been practicing to help you identify the main idea.

1. Paragraph 3 is mainly about:
   (a)   the car journey to the picnic.
   (b)   a new picnic place.
   (c)   the car journey home from the picnic.
   (d)   looking for birds during a picnic.

2. What is the main idea of paragraph 1?
   (a)   It was a warm and sunny day.
   (b)   Everyone wanted to go on a picnic.
   (c)   No one wanted to go on a picnic.
   (d)   Everyone began to cheer.

3. Use the text and your ideas to answer the following:
   (a)   What is the title of the text?

   _____

   (b)   A good title often tells the main idea.

   Do you think this is a good title?   Yes ◯   No ◯

   (c)   Explain why you think this.

   _____

   _____

   _____

   _____

   (d)   Suggest another title that would be good for this story.

   _____

Identifying the Main Idea

Activity: Read the travel brochure below and complete page 30.

Destination

Kia Ora travel guides of New Zealand

New Zealand

1. ### Where is it?

New Zealand is located in the South Pacific Ocean. Its closest neighbor is Australia. New Zealand is made up of two main islands: North Island and South Island. The capital of New Zealand is Wellington, which can be found on the southern tip of North Island. New Zealand's Maori name is *Aotearoa*, which means "Land of the long, white cloud." This name was given by the legendary discoverer of the islands—a man named Kupe.

2. ### History

Maori warrior

The indigenous people of New Zealand are known as the Maori people. They traveled from Polynesia in boats over 1,000 years ago. They settled along the coast. Over the next few hundred years, more and more people from the Polynesian islands traveled to New Zealand to make it their home.

3. Abel Tasman, a Dutch navigator, was the first European to sight New Zealand in 1642. It wasn't until 1769 that British explorer Captain James Cook, claimed New Zealand for Britain and circumnavigated the islands to draw a detailed map. In 1840, New Zealand became a British colony. After this, many British people traveled to New Zealand to make it their home.

Map of New Zealand—"The land of the long, white cloud"

4. ### The Climate

New Zealand has a temperate climate with four seasons: summer, autumn, winter, and spring. Summer is warm and perfect for outdoor activities like swimming, surfing, and hiking. Winter brings rain or snow, which is ideal for skiing and snowboarding.

5. ### The Land

New Zealand is home to many different landscapes. It is surrounded by beautiful, sandy beaches. It also has huge mountains, beautiful volcanoes, and lush subtropical forests. The large glaciers and fjords also add extra-special beauty—the variety of landscapes is amazing!

Because of its beauty, New Zealand has been used as a backdrop for many movies, including *Lord of the Rings* and *The Lion, the Witch and the Wardrobe*.

Name _____

Use the strategies you learned and practiced in *Our Family Outing* to help you find the main idea.

> **Remember:**
> - All the information given in the answers is usually in the text, so you need to ask yourself, "Which answer tells what it is mainly about?"
> - Look at the title, too.
> - Read all the possible answers carefully before making a decision.

1. What is the main idea of paragraph 3?

   (a)   the first people to settle in New Zealand

   (b)   the first map drawn of New Zealand

   (c)   early holidays in New Zealand

   (d)   how New Zealand became a British colony

> **Think!**
> Which answer tells what it is mainly about and links all the ideas?

2. Explain the main idea of the travel brochure.

   _____

   _____

   _____

3. What is the main idea of the final paragraph?

   (a)   New Zealand is so beautiful, it is being used as scenery in movies.

   (b)   New Zealand has lots of famous actors.

   (c)   Everyone in New Zealand likes to watch movies.

   (d)   *The Lion, the Witch and the Wardrobe* was filmed in New Zealand.

4. Look at the subheadings in gray on the travel brochure and answer the following:

   (a)   Do you think "The Land" was a good subheading for the last two paragraphs and described the main ideas?   Yes ◯   No ◯

   (b)   Suggest another good subheading to be used in its place.

   _____

Name _____

Activity: Read the passage below, and use pages 32–34 to show how well you can understand words, find information, and identify main ideas.

Imagine what our bodies would be like if we didn't have skin to hold everything together. Skin is our body's largest organ. It is incredible—it grows with us, protects us, gives us our sense of touch, and helps to keep us warm or cool.

The skin is made up of three layers:

1. The Epidermis

This is the part we can see. But, did you know the skin you see is dead? Underneath that dead layer of skin cells, new skin cells are being made.

This layer also makes melanin. This gives your skin its color. The more melanin your skin cells make, the darker the skin. Melanin also helps to protect your skin from the harmful rays of the sun.

2. The Dermis

This layer is hidden under the epidermis. It contains:

- nerve endings that give us our sense of touch

- blood vessels that keep our skin cells healthy and full of oxygen

- sebaceous (oil) glands to keep our skin lubricated and protected

- sweat glands.

3. The Subcutaneous Layer

This is the bottom layer. It is made up mostly of fat. It helps to keep us warm and absorbs any knocks and bumps we might have. This layer helps to hold the skin onto the rest of our body.

It is important to look after our skin. It needs to be kept clean, so washing it with warm, soapy water is a really good way to keep it healthy. We should also protect our skin from the harmful rays of the sun. Wearing sunscreen, a hat, and protective clothing helps to keep our skin healthy.

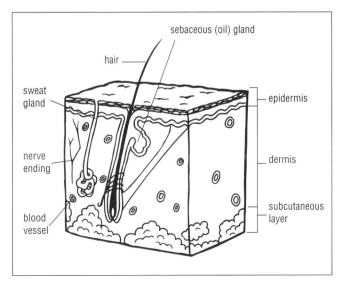

Name _____

> **Remember:**
> - Find the word or phrase in the text.
> - Read that sentence and some of the sentences around it to help you to figure out the meaning.
> - Substitute the word in the sentence with each answer choice to see if it sounds correct.
> - Always check all possible answers before making a decision.

1. What does the word **protect** mean?
   - (a) to wear clothes
   - (b) to cover or shield from injury or danger
   - (c) to keep clean
   - (d) to fight away any danger

2. Explain what **absorbs** means in **absorbs any knocks and bumps**.

   _____

   _____

   _____

3. What does the word **lubricated** mean?
   - (a) wet
   - (b) dry
   - (c) oily
   - (d) soaked

4. Choose the best meaning for the word **harmful**.
   - (a) something that could hurt us
   - (b) something very safe
   - (c) long and hot
   - (d) a part of the sun

5. Draw a picture to show the meaning of **layers**.

Finding Information

Name _____

> **Remember:**
> - Look in the text to find information.
> - Underline keywords in the question to make sure that you know what information you need.
> - Find the keywords in the text, and read the information around them carefully.
> - Always check all possible answers before making a decision.

1. What is the name of the skin we can see?
   - (a) the subcutaneous layer
   - (b) melanin
   - (c) the epidermis
   - (d) the dermis

2. Explain the best way to keep your skin healthy.

   _____

   _____

   _____

3. What gives your skin its color?
   - (a) melanin
   - (b) a sun tan
   - (c) dead skin cells
   - (d) blood vessels

4. Which part of the skin gives us our sense of touch?
   - (a) sweat glands
   - (b) oil glands
   - (c) blood vessels
   - (d) nerve endings

5. Do you think you have:

   | a large | a little | a medium | amount of melanin in your skin?

   Explain. _____

   _____

Name _____

> **Remember:**
> - The main idea links all the other ideas together and tells what the text is about.
> - The title is an excellent clue to the main idea of the text.
> - Always check all possible answers before making a decision.

1. What is the main idea of the last paragraph?
   (a)   tells us about the harmful rays of the sun
   (b)   tells us how to wash our skin
   (c)   it explains how to care for and protect our skin to keep it healthy
   (d)   explains what to wear when playing outside

2. Explain the main idea of the opening paragraph in gray.

   _____

   _____

   _____

   _____

3. Use the text and your ideas to answer the following:
   (a)   What is the title of the text?

   _____

   (b)   A good title often tells the main idea.

   Do you think this is a good title?   Yes ◯   No ◯

   (c)   Explain why you think this.

   _____

   _____

   _____

   (d)   Suggest another title that would be suitable.

   _____

Sequencing

Lesson Objective

- Students will sequence events.

Background Information

This section demonstrates how to determine the order in which events occur, sometimes using time markers and other strategies to identify the relationship between events.

Knowing the sequence of events is an important and often critical factor in a reader's understanding of a text.

First, students need to determine from the question which events they are required to sequence. Then, they should locate them in the text and look for any time-marker words that could be helpful. Examples could include: *before, then, when, while, after, finally, at last,* or *following*.

Students may also find creating timelines of sections of the text or specific events a useful strategy.

Activity Answers

Diary of Ben's Tennis Ball .... **Pages 39–42**

- Practice Page: Page 41
  1. (b)
  2. Ben took his water bottle out of his backpack.
  3. (d)
- On Your Own: Page 42
  1. (c)
  2. (a) 3
     (b) 5
     (c) 1
     (d) 4
     (e) 2
  3. Ben went over a bump.
  4. (a) after   (b) before   (c) after

The Life Cycle of a Silkworm .... **Pages 43–44**

- Try It Out: Page 44
  1. (d)
  2. (a) 4
     (b) 3
     (c) 2
     (d) 5
  3. It lays eggs, then it dies.
  4. (a) before
     (b) after

Assessment Answers

Sequencing...**Page 58**

  1. (a)
  2. They all went to meet some of the other families.
  3. (d)

Lesson Objective

• Students will compare and contrast people, places, and events.

Background Information

The ability to compare and contrast the information provided in a text enhances the reader's understanding of that text and is an important comprehension skill students need to practice.

Students are required to categorize information in order to determine what some people, places, and events have in common or how they differ.

Graphic organizers are very useful tools for identifying similarities and differences, particularly Venn diagrams, T–charts, and compare-and-contrast charts.

same	different

T-chart

A	B	A	B
compare		contrast	

Compare-and-Contrast chart

Activity Answers

Delicious Drinks .... **Pages 45–48**
• Practice Page: Page 47
   1. (c)
   2. (a) Sugar only: Honey Lemon Drink, Ice cream only: Banana Milkshake, Both: Chocolate Delight
      (b) Fruit Punch
   3. They both use fruit and ice cubes.
   4. Answers will vary.
• On Your Own: Page 48
   1. (b)
   2. (a) honey, banana, and yogurt
      (b) milk/ice cream/ice cubes
      (c) Both of the drinks serve two people; both served cold
   3. Fruit Punch and Honey Lemon Drink
   4. Banana Milkshake, Honey Lemon Drink, and Fruit Punch

Turtles/Tortoises .... **Pages 49–50**
• Try It Out: Page 50
   1. (a) **Turtles:** flat shells, long legs, live mostly in water, webbed feet
        Tortoises: dome-shaped shells, short, stumpy legs, live on land, stumpy feet
      (b) mostly in water; on land
      (c) flat; dome-shaped
      (d) long; short, stumpy
      (e) webbed; stumpy
   2. Both are mostly found in warm to hot areas/ Not found in Antarctica
   3. Answers will vary.

Assessment Answers

Finding Similarities and Differences ....**Page 59**
   1. (c)
   2. The children had more room. Their cousin Jade didn't come. The trip was less noisy.
   3. **Lilac Lake:** Braden whined more in car, tent near children same age, lots of things to do, Braden needed a piggyback ride, it rained
      Roper River: shorter trip, tent near children same age, girl with same name, lots of things to do, lots of mosquitoes
      (a) Tent near children same age, lots of things to do
      (b) Answers will vary.

Predicting

Lesson Objective

• Students will use information from a text to predict outcomes not explicitly stated in the text.

Background Information

To be able to predict outcomes, often in terms of the probable actions or reactions of specific characters, students need to focus on content and understand what they read. They need to monitor their understanding as they read, constantly confirming, rejecting, or adjusting their predictions.

The focus of this section is on teaching students how to locate and use the information provided in the text to determine probable outcomes and then to evaluate their predictions.

Students need to be able to locate specific information related to an issue and/or characters, using keywords and concepts. Their predictions should not be wild guesses, but well-thought-out, relevant ideas based on the information provided and some prior knowledge.

If students' answers differ, it is suggested that they check again to see why their answer varies from the one given. If they can justify their answer, teachers may decide to accept it.

Activity Answers

The Mushroom Hunt ....**Pages 51–54**

• Practice Page: Page 53
   1. (c)
   2. Gran would probably have made them mushrooms on toast.
   3. (d)
   4. Answers will vary. Answers could indicate that Brooke was happy to see all the mushrooms Leah picked.
• On Your Own: Page 54
   1. (a) Yes. Answers could indicate that they saw a lot more mushrooms in the top field than those closer to the house, so it would be a good idea. Answers may vary.
   2. (b)
   3. No. The text says Leah was impatient and she raced ahead and did things without thinking. Also, Brooke sorted the mushrooms out properly on the sheet.
   4. Gran will probably check again.

The Story of Momotaro ....**Pages 55–56**

• Try It Out: Page 56
   1. (d)
   2. (a)
   3. They will row their boat.
   4. Answers will vary.

Assessment Answers

Predicting ....**Page 60**

   1. (b)
   2. (c)
   3. Answers will vary.
   4. Answers will vary.

Helpful Hints

SEQUENCING

- Make sure you know which events you need to sequence. Then find those events in the text.

- Pay attention to how they are related. Making a mental picture of what is happening in the text sometimes helps you imagine the sequence.

- Always check all possible answers before deciding on your answer.

FINDING SIMILARITIES AND DIFFERENCES

- Make sure you understand the question before you begin. Then find the keywords.

- Use a chart, table, Venn diagram, or other type of organizer, if you need to. This will help you find similarities and differences.

- Always check all possible answers before deciding on your answer.

PREDICTING

- You need to find the information that connects to the question.

- The answer will not be found in the text, but there is information you can use and think about as you read. The writer will suggest, rather than tell, what is likely to happen. You must use the details in the text to help you predict.

- Always check all possible answers before deciding on your answer.

Name _____

To fully understand what you read, you must be able to determine the order in which events happened. This is called sequencing.

Activity: Read the diary entry below and complete pages 40–42.

Diary of Ben's Tennis Ball
Saturday, May 25

1. All week, as usual, I had spent my days in a plastic tub, but Saturday was Ben's tennis day. I could hear the dishes being put into the dishwasher and knew that breakfast was over. Next, I heard Ben's footsteps hurrying down the hall and the door being opened. He put me into a backpack with his tennis racket, sneakers, clean socks (fortunately), a bottle of cold water, an orange, and a towel.

2. We all bobbled around in the backpack as Ben rode his bike to the tennis courts. I was feeling cold and squashed up next to the water bottle. Was I glad when I landed on top of the towel when Ben went over a big bump!

3. At the tennis courts, I was gently tapped by the racket a little ways into the air before I landed back on the racket and bounced back up again. This was a warm-up exercise. Now for the real thing! This time I was whacked over a net and landed on the other side. Ben's partner's racket hit me back. Ouch! At least I was getting some exercise in the fresh air.

4. I didn't like it when Ben hit me, and I went headfirst into the net. He had to grab hold of me tightly to squeeze me out of the hole I was stuck in. Another time, I was hit so hard I eventually ended up at the back of the courts, where a large puddle was waiting for me. It wasn't so bad getting wet, as I was pretty hot by this time!

5. When we finally got home, Ben took his water bottle out of his backpack and left the rest of us in the backpack next to his bike. Unfortunately, he left the zipper open. Shortly afterwards, I heard a snuffling noise and then saw a wet nose sniffing in the bag. Rufus, Ben's dog, had sniffed me out! He loves balls. I spent 15 minutes in a warm, wet mouth between teeth that were poking into me. He dropped me now and then, sometimes on the grass and other times in the itchy sand.

6. At last, Rufus got tired and dropped me near the trash can. I rolled behind it to hide. I would much rather be next to a smelly trash can until Ben found me than covered in dog drool!

Name _____

Follow the steps below to learn how to sequence events. The order in which things happen is very important.

> - Make sure you understand which events you need to sequence.
> - Look in the text to find the events listed as possible answers and underline them.
> - You will need to determine how these events are related. There may be some time-marker words, such as *then*, *before*, or *next*, in the text to help you.
> - Always check all possible answers before making a decision.

1. Which event happened *after* the tennis ball was squashed up next to the water bottle in the backpack?

   (a) The dishes were put into the dishwasher.

   (b) The ball heard Ben's footsteps hurrying down the hall.

   (c) The ball was put into Ben's backpack.

   (d) The ball landed on top of the towel.

2. Choose the best answer. Think about each choice carefully.

   (a) This happened before Ben put things into his backpack, so it is not the right answer.

   (b) Ben hurried down the hall to get his backpack. This is not a good answer.

   (c) The ball couldn't feel squashed before it was put into the backpack. This is not a good answer.

   (d) This happened when they went over a bump *after* the ball felt squashed. This is the right answer.

1. Which event happened *just before* the tennis ball saw a wet nose sniffing in the bag that had been left outside?

   (a) The ball got stuck in the net.

   (b) Ben left the zipper of the backpack open.

   (c) The ball heard a snuffling noise.

   (d) The ball was dropped in the sand.

2. Choose the best answer. Think about each choice carefully.

   (a) The ball was stuck in the net while Ben was still at the club, so this is probably not the right answer.

   (b) Ben left the backpack open when he took out the water bottle. This could be the right answer. But did it happen *just before*?

   (c) The ball heard the dog snuffling, trying to get into the bag before seeing the wet nose. This is a better answer than (b) and seems to be right. Remember, you must check all the answers.

   (d) The ball was out of the bag in the dog's mouth when this happened, so it is not the right answer.

Sequencing

Name _____

Use the strategies you learned to practice sequencing. Use the clues in the "Think!" boxes to help you.

1. Which happened **first**?

   (a) The tennis ball was hit by Ben's partner's racket.

   (b) The tennis ball bobbled around in the backpack.

   (c) The tennis ball landed in a puddle.

   (d) The tennis ball went over a bump.

> **Think!**
> You will need to find and underline all of the answers in the text to determine which one happened first.

2. What was the **first** thing Ben did when he got home from tennis practice?

   _____

   _____

> **Think!**
> The rest of the sentence will give you a clue.

3. Which one of these events should be listed as Event 2 in the box below?

   (a) The tennis ball was whacked over the net.

   (b) The tennis ball landed on the towel.

   (c) The tennis ball did a warm-up exercise.

   (d) The tennis ball heard dishes being put into the dishwasher.

> **Think!**
> Read Events 1, 3, and 4, then try to determine which event is missing.

Event 1.	The tennis ball was in the plastic tub.	
Event 2.	_____	
Event 3.	The tennis ball heard footsteps in the hall.	
Event 4.	The tennis ball was put into the backpack.	

On Your Own

Name _____

Use the strategies you have been practicing to help you determine the sequence of events.

1. What happened *just after* Ben hit the ball into the net?
    (a)   The ball was whacked back over the net.
    (b)   The ball rolled into a puddle.
    (c)   The ball was squeezed out of the net.
    (d)   Ben hit the ball with his racket.

2. List these events in order from 1 to 5.

    (a)   The ball was in the dog's mouth .... ☐

    (b)   The ball rolled behind the trash can .... ☐

    (c)   Ben left the zipper of the backpack open .... ☐

    (d)   Rufus dropped the ball in the sand .... ☐

    (e)   Rufus put his nose into the bag .... ☐

3. Explain what happened *between* these two events.
    •   The ball was feeling cold and squashed up next to the water bottle.

    •   _____

    •   The ball was on top of the towel.

4. Write either the word *before* or *after* to complete the sentences.

    (a)   The ball rolled into a puddle _____ Ben hit it into the net.

    (b)   The ball was cold and squashed _____ Ben went over the bump.

    (c)   The ball hid behind the trash can _____ Rufus got tired.

Name _____

Activity: Read the text below and complete page 44.

The Life Cycle of a Silkworm

Follow this explanation about the life cycle of a silkworm moth.

- A female adult silkworm moth lays between 200 and 500 tiny eggs.

- Adult moths have fat bodies and small wings. They lay eggs. They cannot fly or eat and will die within five days.

- The eggs are light yellow at first then turn black after a few days.

- After three weeks, the moth breaks out of the silk cocoon.

- About 20 days after they are laid, the eggs hatch into tiny caterpillars.

- The caterpillar changes into a moth inside the cocoon.

- The caterpillars eat fresh mulberry leaves day and night.

- Then, the caterpillars stop eating. Each one starts to spin a cocoon of silk around itself.

- They grow quickly and molt (shed their skin) several times before they are fully grown.

Name _____

Use the strategies you learned and practiced in *Diary of Ben's Tennis Ball* to help you determine the sequence of events.

Remember:
- Make sure you understand which events you need to sequence.
- Look in the text to find the events listed as possible answers and underline them.
- Pay attention to how these events are related. There may be some time-marker words, such as *then, before, next*, etc.
- Always check all possible answers before making a decision.

---

1. Which event happens **soon after** the eggs hatch?
   (a) The caterpillar spins a cocoon.
   (b) The adult moth dies.
   (c) The eggs are laid.
   (d) The caterpillar eats mulberry leaves.

> **Think!**
> Read the steps in the text and determine which one comes first.

2. List the events in order from 1 to 5. The first one has been done for you.

   Between 200 and 500 eggs are laid. `1`

   (a) The caterpillar changes into a moth. ☐

   (b) The caterpillar stops eating. ☐

   (c) The eggs turn black. ☐

   (d) The moth breaks out of the cocoon. ☐

3. Explain what happens to the moth **after** it breaks out of the silk cocoon.

   _____

   _____

4. Write the word **before** or **after** to complete the sentence.

   (a) The caterpillars molt several times _____ they are fully grown.

   (b) The caterpillars spin a silk cocoon _____ they stop eating.

Finding Similarities and Differences

Name _____

To help you understand what you read in a text, you sometimes need to think about how things are alike or how they are different and make comparisons.

Activity: Read the drink recipes below and complete pages 46–48.

• • • • • • • • • • • • Delicious Drinks • • • • • • • • • • • •

Which of the drinks below would you most like to make? Perhaps you would like to make all of them!

Banana Milkshake

$1\frac{1}{2}$ cups milk

1 banana chopped into slices

1 tablespoon honey

1 tablespoon plain yogurt

1 scoop of ice cream

ice cubes

Put all ingredients into a blender. Blend until smooth. Serves 2.

Fruit Punch

$2\frac{1}{2}$ cups orange juice

$2\frac{1}{2}$ cups pineapple juice

3 cups lemonade

chopped fruit of choice

ice cubes

Put all ingredients into a large bowl or jug. Stir with a ladel. Serves 8.

Chocolate Delight

2 tablespoons chocolate-milk mix

2 tablespoons sugar

$\frac{1}{4}$ cup warm water

2 cups cold milk

2 scoops of ice cream

cocoa powder to sprinkle

ice cubes

Dissolve chocolate-milk mix and sugar in warm water. Pour into two large glasses. Add 1 cup of milk, a scoop of ice cream, and ice cubes to each glass. Sprinkle with cocoa. Serves 2.

Honey Lemon Drink

1 cup water

2 teaspoons honey

1 teaspoon freshly squeezed lemon juice

1 teaspoon sugar

Pour water and honey into a cup. Heat in the microwave for 1 minute and 30 seconds. Stir in lemon and sugar. Serves 1.

Learning Page

Name _____

Follow the steps below to learn how you can organize information to make it easier to answer questions about similarities and differences.

- Make sure you understand the question and underline the keywords.
- Sometimes it is easy to see how things are different or the same if you are comparing two things. However, if there are three or more things to compare, it can be helpful to organize the information in a chart. Two examples are shown below.
- Always check all possible answers before making a decision.

1. Which two recipes use milk?

   (a) Fruit Punch and Banana Milkshake.

   (b) Chocolate Delight and Honey Lemon Drink.

   (c) Honey Lemon Drink and Fruit Punch.

   (d) Banana Milkshake and Chocolate Delight.

Milk	No Milk

2. Choose the best answer.

   You will find it helpful to write each recipe name in a column in the chart above.

   (a) Fruit Punch does not use milk, but Banana Milkshake does. This is not the right answer.

   (b) Chocolate Delight uses milk, but Honey Lemon Drink does not. This is not the right answer.

   (c) Neither of these uses milk. This is not the right answer.

   (d) Both of these drinks use milk. This is the right answer.

---

1. Which recipe uses honey and water?

   (a) Fruit Punch

   (b) Chocolate Delight

   (c) Banana Milkshake

   (d) Honey Lemon Drink

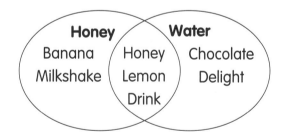

2. Choose the best answer.

   If you look at the Venn diagram, you can see that:

   (a) Fruit Punch is not in the diagram because it does not use honey or water. This is not the right answer.

   (b) Chocolate Delight is in the *Water* section only. This is not the right answer.

   (c) Banana Milkshake is in the *Honey* section only. This is not the right answer.

   (d) Honey Lemon Drink is in the *Honey* and *Water* section. This is the right answer.

Finding Similarities and Differences

Name _____

Use the strategies you learned to practice finding similarities and differences.

1. Which recipe has both sugar and ice cream? Complete the chart to help answer this question.

   (a) Banana Milkshake

   (b) Fruit Punch

   (c) Chocolate Delight

   (d) Honey Lemon Drink

Sugar	Ice Cream

2. (a) Use a Venn diagram to show the information you found to answer Question 1.

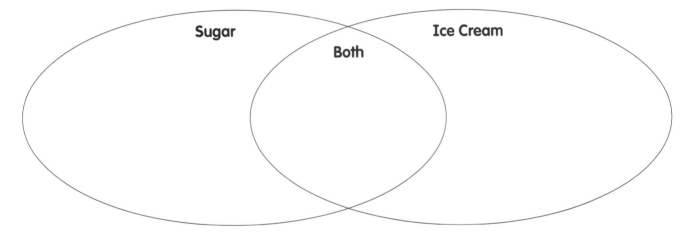

   (b) Which recipe was not in your Venn diagram? _____

3. What are two ways Banana Milkshake and Fruit Punch are alike?

   _____

   _____

4. What are two ways Chocolate Delight and Honey Lemon Drink are different?

   _____

   _____

Name _____

Use the strategies you have been practicing to help you identify similarities and differences.

1. Which drink is different because it needs a machine to mix it?

   (a) Fruit Punch
   (b) Banana Milkshake

   (c) Honey Lemon Drink
   (d) Chocolate Delight

2. Answer the questions about the information shown on the Venn diagram.

   Banana Milkshake
   honey
   banana
   yogurt

   milk
   ice cream
   ice cubes
   serves 2

   Chocolate Delight
   sugar
   water
   chocolate-milk mix
   cocoa

   (a) Three ingredients that are in Banana Milkshake and not in Chocolate Delight

   are _____, _____,

   and _____.

   (b) Name two ingredients that are in both drinks.

   _____ and _____

   (c) There is something that these drinks have in common that is not an ingredient. What is it?

   _____

3. There are two drinks that need to be stirred. What are they?

   _____ and _____

4. Which three drinks have fruit juice or pieces of fruit in them?

   _____, _____,

   and _____

Name _____

Activity: Read the passages below and complete page 50.

Turtles

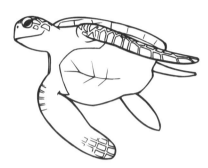

1. Turtles are reptiles. Reptiles have scales, breathe air, and lay eggs. They are also cold-blooded, which means their body is the same temperature as the air or water around them. Turtles are mostly found in warm to hot areas of the world. The only continent they are not found on is Antarctica.

2. Both turtles and tortoises are the only reptiles with a shell. Many turtles can pull their head, legs, and tail inside their shell to protect themselves from enemies. Turtles usually have a flat type of shell.

3. Turtles spend most of their life in water. They have long legs and webbed feet to help them swim. Turtles that live in the sea also have flippers. Most turtles eat both plants and meat. They do not have teeth but have a kind of beak they use for biting.

4. Female turtles lay eggs on land and bury them in soil or sand. When the females have laid their eggs, they do not look after them. After the eggs hatch, the tiny turtles, called *hatchlings*, must look after themselves.

Tortoises

1. Tortoises are reptiles. Reptiles have scales, breathe air, and lay eggs. They are also cold-blooded, which means their body is the same temperature as the air or water around them. Tortoises are mostly found in warm to hot areas of the world. The only continent they are not found on is Antarctica.

2. Both tortoises and turtles are the only reptiles with a shell. Many tortoises can pull their head, legs, and tail inside their shell to protect themselves from enemies. Tortoises usually have a dome-shaped type of shell.

3. Tortoises spend their life on land. They have short, stumpy legs and feet. Most tortoises eat both plants and meat. They do not have teeth but have a kind of beak they use for biting.

4. Female tortoises lay eggs on land and bury them in soil or sand. When the females have laid their eggs, they do not look after them. After the eggs hatch, the tiny tortoises, called *hatchlings*, must look after themselves.

Name _____

Use the strategies you learned and practiced in *Delicious Drinks* to help you recognize similarities and differences.

Remember:
- Make sure you understand the question and underline the keywords.
- Sometimes it is easy to see how things are different or the same if you are comparing two things. However, if there are three or more things to compare, it can be helpful to organize the information in a chart.
- Always check all the possible answers before making a decision.

Think!
Try to find each answer in both parts of the text.

1. (a) Complete the chart by marking an **X** in the correct boxes. Then answer the questions below.

	dome-shaped shells	flat shells	long legs	short, stumpy legs	live mostly in water	live on land	stumpy feet	webbed feet
Most turtles								
Most tortoises								

(b) Turtles live _____

and tortoises live _____.

(c) Turtles have _____ shells

and tortoises have _____ shells.

(d) Turtles have _____ legs and tortoises have

_____ legs.

(e) Turtles have _____ feet and tortoises have

_____ feet.

2. What is one thing the same about where turtles and tortoises can be found?

_____

3. Write something else the same about turtles and tortoises.

_____

Name _____

As we read, it is important to pay attention to what is happening and to think about what may happen.

Activity: Read the story below and complete pages 52–54.

The Mushroom Hunt

1. My sister and I were staying at our grandparents' farm for a week because we didn't have school. The first really heavy autumn rains had been falling all week. This meant mushrooms were sprouting all over the farm. We'd decided to walk up to the top field to pick some. I'd packed some plastic bags, some scissors, a bottle of water, some fruit, and a plastic sheet.

2. "Hurry up, Brooke," my younger sister shouted impatiently to me.

3. "OK, Leah," I answered. "I just want to check that we have everything for our mushroom hunt."

4. After putting on our raincoats, we set off along the muddy track that leads to the top field. Gran waved goodbye and said to remember to watch where we walked. When we reached the first fence, Leah wanted to duck between the wires to get to the other side. I suggested we walk down to the gate and climb over because some of the fence had barbed wire.

5. Eventually, we arrived at the top field. There were heaps more mushrooms there than in the field close to the house. Some were so big that Gran would only need to cook a couple to put on a piece of toast for a yummy breakfast! Gran had said to be careful not to get mushrooms and toadstools mixed up because toadstools are poisonous. Mushrooms have a flatter cap and are a dusky pink color underneath. I looked carefully before picking each one.

6. We took a break and sat on the sheet while I sorted out the mushrooms properly. Leah suddenly spied a group of mushrooms on the other side of a boggy area in the field. She jumped up and started to race over.

7. "Don't go too close to the bog!" I warned her.

8. Five minutes later, Leah returned with her arms full of mushrooms—but was she a mess! I wonder what Gran will say when she sees her!

Name _____

Follow the steps below to learn how to make a prediction about what may happen.

- The answers are not in the text.
- Find information in the text to use and think about.
- You need to find information related to the question. (This could be underlined.)
- Think hard! What is the writer suggesting might happen?
- Always consider all possible answers before making a decision.

1. The girls put on their raincoats. What did they think might happen?

   (a) It would get cold.

   (b) There might be thunder.

   (c) It would be windy.

   (d) It might rain.

2. Choose the best answer. Think about each choice carefully.

   (a) A raincoat could stop them from feeling cold, but the text does not talk about the weather being cold. This may not be the best answer.

   (b) There is no talk of thunder in the text. This is not the best answer.

   (c) There is no talk about it being windy in the text. This is not the best answer.

   (d) The text says that heavy autumn rains had been falling, so the girls would think it might rain. This is the best answer.

1. How will Leah probably feel when she gets back to the farm looking like a mess?

   (a) hungry

   (b) hot and bored

   (c) worried about what Gran will say

   (d) very happy

2. Choose the best answer. Think about each choice carefully.

   (a) Leah could be hungry, but it doesn't say anything about it in the text. This is probably not the best answer.

   (b) There is nothing about it being hot in the text. Probably not the best answer.

   (c) Gran told them to be careful. Leah wasn't careful, and Brooke was wondering what Gran would say. This is a good answer.

   (d) Leah wouldn't be feeling happy about being a mess. Not a good answer.

Predicting

Name _____

Use the strategies you learned to practice making predictions about what will happen. Use the clues in the "Think!" boxes to help you.

1. What might have happened if the girls had ducked between the wires instead of walking down to the gate?

    (a)   They wouldn't have reached the top field.

    (b)   They could have found more mushrooms.

    (c)   They could have snagged their raincoats on the wire.

    (d)   They would have had to walk farther to reach the top field.

> **Think!**
> Read the last sentence in paragraph 4.

2. Imagine the girls are having breakfast the next day. What might Gran have made for them?

    _____

    _____

    _____

    _____

> **Think!**
> Read paragraph 5.

3. What will Gran probably say when Leah comes back from the mushroom hunt in such a mess?

    (a)   "Did you find any toadstools?"

    (b)   "Did you get wet, Leah?"

    (c)   "Wasn't the thunder loud?"

    (d)   "I told you to watch where you were walking, Leah."

> **Think!**
> What did Gran say when she waved goodbye to the girls?

4. How might have Brooke reacted when she saw Leah?

    _____

    _____

    _____

> **Think!**
> Read paragraph 8.

Name _____

Use the strategies you have been practicing to help you make predictions.

1. Do you think the girls would go all the way to the top field again to collect mushrooms?

   Yes ◯   No ◯

   Explain why you think this.

   _____

   _____

   _____

2. Imagine Leah sees another pile of mushrooms near the bog. What might she do this time?
   (a)   She'll walk through the bog to get them.
   (b)   She'll walk carefully around the bog to get them.
   (c)   She'll use her grandfather's tractor to get them.
   (d)   She'll ask Brooke to give her a piggyback ride to get them.

3. Gran had explained the difference between mushrooms and toadstools to the girls. Brooke looked carefully to check. Do you think that Leah did this, too?

   Yes ◯   No ◯

   Explain why you think this.

   _____

   _____

   _____

4. What will Gran most likely do to make sure the girls have picked mushrooms and not toadstools?

   _____

   _____

   _____

Predicting

Name _____

Activity: Read the Japanese legend below and complete page 56.

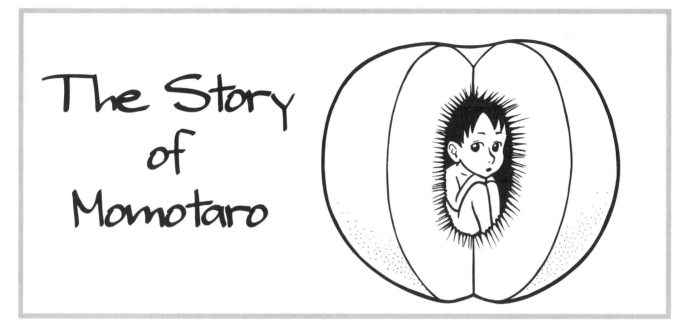

The Story of Momotaro

1.   Once upon a time, an old man and an old woman were washing their clothes in a stream. Suddenly, the old woman noticed an enormous peach floating by. They grabbed the peach and took it home to eat.

2.   When they cut into the peach to eat it, they were surprised to find a sweet, little boy inside. The old man and the old lady were so happy. At last, they had a child of their own. They decided to call him Momotaro.

3.   As time went by, Momotaro grew big and strong. He was kind and thoughtful and was always ready to help anyone.

4.   Not far from the village where Momotaro lived was an island called Onigashima. On this island lived some nasty ogres. They had been frightening the villagers and taking their treasures. Momotaro decided to stop the ogres from doing this. His father gave him a sword, and his mother gave him some millet dumplings to eat on his journey.

5.   On the way to the island, Momotaro met a dog, a bird, and a monkey. He asked them to help him fight the ogres. They agreed, as long as Momotaro would give them some of his millet dumplings. The dumplings they ate gave them the strength of a thousand people.

6.   After rowing to the island, they went in search of the ogres. The monkey scratched them, the bird pecked them, the dog bit them, and Momotaro used his sword. The ogres surrendered and gave Momotaro all the treasures they had stolen.

Name _____

Use the strategies you learned and practiced in *The Mushroom Hunt* to help you make predictions.

Remember:
- The answers are usually not in the text, so you can't just read them, but there is information for you to use and think about.
- You need to find information related to the question. (This could be underlined.)
- Think hard! What is the writer suggesting might happen?
- Always consider all possible answers before making a decision.

1. What will Momotaro most likey do with all the treasure?

   (a)   Give it back to the ogres if they say *sorry*.

   (b)   Bury it in the sand on the island.

   (c)   Keep it for himself.

   (d)   Return it to the villagers.

Think!
Read paragraphs 3 and 4 to help you decide which answer to choose.

2. The next time Momotaro goes on an adventure, what is he more likely to take with him?

   (a)   millet dumplings

   (b)   the ogres

   (c)   some treasure

   (d)   a peach

3. How do you think Momotaro and the animals will get off the island?

   _____

   _____

4. Imagine that Momotaro had met an elephant on the way. What do you think the elephant would have done to the ogres?

   _____

   _____

   _____

Name _____

Activity: Read the passage below, and use pages 58–60 to show how well you can sequence, find similarities and differences, and predict.

The Foster Family's Camping Trip

1. During summer break, I went with my family on our yearly camping trip. We camped at Roper River, which is a lot closer than Lilac Lake, where we stayed last year.

2. After helping to pack the car, we set off at about eight o'clock. My brother, Braden, and I had more room in the back of our car this time as my cousin, Jade, wasn't with us. Mom said the trip was a lot less noisy with only one boy and a girl!

3. It only took two and a half hours to drive to the Roper River campsite. Braden didn't whine as much as last year, which was great. We stopped to stretch our legs along the way, while Dad filled up the car with gas.

4. When we got there, we helped to unpack and set up the tent. Then, we all went to meet some other families. The same as last year, our tent was pitched near one with a boy and a girl about our ages. I found out that her name was the same as mine—Sophie! Her brother's name was Cade.

5. Like at Lilac Lake, there were so many things to do. The first afternoon we went for a hike around the lake. Braden didn't need a piggyback ride from Dad this year, but he began to grumble when he walked through some loose gravel and said his heel was hurting.

6. The next day, we rented canoes to use on the lake. First, Mom and I got in our canoe. We did very well in our canoe, but Dad had trouble with Braden in theirs. Braden kept leaning over too far to look at the things in the water. Mom and I lost sight of them around a bend in the river. Unfortunately, we heard a loud splash and shouting, and we guessed what had happened!

7. We went fishing for trout every morning, swimming most afternoons when it was warmer, played with our new friends, and had a yummy barbeque every night. Unlike Lake Lilac, it didn't rain at all, but there were lots of mosquitoes to annoy us. Still, I was sad to leave.

Name _____

Remember:

- Make sure you understand which events you need to sequence.
- Look in the text to find the events listed as possible answers and underline them.
- Pay attention to how these events are related. Look for time-marker words, such as *then*, *before*, *next*, etc.
- Always check all possible answers before making a decision.

1. Which event happened second?

    (a)   The Fosters set off on their trip.

    (b)   Dad stopped for gas.

    (c)   The family packed the car.

    (d)   They arrived at Roper River.

2. What did the family do after they set up the tent?

    _____

    _____

3. Which one of these events should be listed as Event 3 in the box below?

    (a)   Sophie and her Mom heard a splash.

    (b)   The family went hiking.

    (c)   Braden began to grumble on the hike.

    (d)   Braden kept leaning over in the canoe to look in the water.

Event 1.	The Fosters rented two canoes.
Event 2.	Sophie and her Mom got in their canoe.
Event 3.	_____
Event 4.	Sophie and her Mom went around a bend in the river.

Name _____

Remember:
- Make sure you understand the question, and underline the keywords.
- Use a chart or diagram if you need it.
- Always check all possible answers before making a decision.

---

1. What do the Fosters do the same every year?

   (a)   go trout fishing

   (b)   rent canoes

   (c)   go camping

   (d)   go to Roper River

2. Read paragraph 2 and list three things that were different from the trip the family took the year before.

   _____

   _____

3. Complete the chart by marking an **X** in the correct boxes. Then answer the questions below.

	Shorter trip	Braden whined more in car	Tent near children same age	Girl with same name	Lots of things to do	Braden needed a piggyback ride	It rained	Lots of mosquitoes
Lake Lilac								
Roper River								

   (a)   Which two things were the same about both trips?

   _____

   _____

   (b)   List two things that were different about both trips.

   _____

   _____

Name _____

Remember:

- You need to find and underline information related to the question.
- The answer is not in the text, but there is information you can use and think about.
- The writer will suggest rather than tell what is likely to happen.
- Always check all possible answers before making a decision.

1. Next time Sophie camps at Roper River, what will she probably take with her?

   (a) umbrella

   (b) mosquito spray

   (c) tennis racket

   (d) canoe

2. Next time Braden goes in a canoe, what will he most likely do?

   (a) stand up

   (b) lean over to look at things

   (c) sit in the middle of the canoe

   (d) jump up and down

3. Imagine that next year the Fosters are deciding whether to go back to Roper River or Lilac Lake for their camping trip. Where do you think they will choose?

   Roper River ⚪   Lilac Lake ⚪

   Explain why.

   _____

   _____

4. If the trip to Roper River had taken five hours, do you think Braden would have whined more?

   Yes ⚪   No ⚪

   Explain your answer.

   _____

   _____

Drawing Conclusions

Lesson Objective

- Students will make judgments and reach conclusions based on facts and/or details provided in a text.

Background Information

This section demonstrates how to decide on the meaning of facts and details provided in a text and how to build up evidence in order to make judgments and reach conclusions about the information.

Students also need to be able to search for evidence to support a particular conclusion by locating the relevant information in the text and then making judgments about it.

In higher-order comprehension skills such as this, answers are not always immediately obvious, and discussion about why one answer is judged to be the best should be encouraged. However, teachers may decide to accept another answer if a student can provide the necessary evidence to support the answer he or she has given.

Activity Answers

Guide Dogs...**Pages 65–68**

- Practice Page: Page 67
  1. (c)
  2. (a)
  3. (d)
  4. Answers should indicate that a guide dog gets used to sudden loud noises and/or being in bad weather outdoors.
- On Your Own: Page 68
  1. (b)
  2. (d)
  3. (a)
  4. Answers should indicate that at eighteen months the dog goes from the puppy raiser to the special trainer, is trained for about four months by him/her and then a month with its master—this takes about two years (twenty-three months).

Ban Cats!..**Pages 69–70**

- Try It Out: Page 70
  1. (b)
  2. The neighborhood cats fighting all night are the main reason the writer gets woken up.
  3. (c)
  4. Answers will vary.

Assessment Answers

Drawing Conclusions...**Page 84**

1. (b)
2. (c)
3. Answers will vary.
4. Answers will vary, but may reference the food grown by farmers.

Lesson Objective

• Students will summarize text by linking important information and identifying the main points.

Background Information

To be able to summarize text successfully, students first need to be clear about what they are being asked to do and what form their answer should take. (For example, a one-word answer or a more detailed explanation may be required.) It will help if they underline the keywords in the question.

They then need to locate any relevant information in the text, underline it, and establish how it is linked. Words such as *while*, *but*, *and*, *when*, and *as* may be significant in establishing how the information is linked. Unnecessary and irrelevant information should be omitted and the main points established for inclusion in the summary.

Students may need to locate information throughout the entire text in order to summarize the main points for some questions.

Answers may vary and will require teacher review. Those given below are provided as a guide to the main points.

Activity Answers

Seahorses .... **Pages 71–74**
  • Practice Page: Page 73
    1. (d)
    2. reefs, seaweed beds, freshwater habitats
    3. (a)
    4. Seahorses swim very slowly upright and mostly up and down.
  • On Your Own: Page 74
    1. (a) horse-shaped
       (b) like an aardvark
       (c) curved, monkey-like
       (d) hard outer covering, little spines
       (e) white, yellow, black, brown, gray, banded, or spotted
    2. (c)
    3. Seahorses use their tail to hold on to sea plants while eating so they won't be swept away.
    4. Seahorses are endangered because of water pollution and being collected.

One of Those Days .... **Pages 75–76**
  • Try It Out: Page 76
    1. (a)
    2. The poet's mom was upset when he forgot to set his alarm and got out of bed late, he spilled juice, and he fought with his brother.
    3. The poet's teacher was upset when he left his homework at home and he talked in class.
    4. These things were: burned the toast, found the jam was used up, spilled juice, sandwiches were soggy from a leaking drink, and no dessert for fighting with his brother.

Assessment Answers

Summarizing .... **Page 85**
    1. (c)
    2. (d)
    3. Poseidon's temple was built from precious metals and had a gold statue of him inside driving six winged horses.
    4. It was destroyed because the people became too greedy, which angered the god, Zeus.

Lesson Objective

• Students will make inferences about what is most likely to be true based on information provided in the text.

Background Information

Inferences are opinions about what is most likely to be true and are formed after careful evaluation of all the available information. Students need to realize that because there is no information that tells them the actual answer, their inferences may not be correct. They have to determine what makes the most sense given the information provided and to then look for details to support their decisions. They may need to use some prior knowledge to help them determine their answer.

The focus of this section is on teaching students how to use contextual information, both written and visual, to determine what they believe to be true. They then must find further evidence to support their decisions.

Student answers will need to be checked by the teacher, but some possible answers have been provided as a guide.

Activity Answers

The Story of King Midas .... **Pages 77–80**

- Practice Page: Page 79
  1. (d)
  2. (c)
  3. He ran around the castle touching things and turning them to gold. Gold made him happy.
  4. No; Answers could include that he only thought for one second before making his wish.
  5. Answers will vary.
- On Your Own: Page 80
  1. (c)
  2. (b)
  3. Possible answer: He wanted to know that Midas was sure about the wish because he didn't think it was a good idea.
  4. Answers will vary.

Surprise Dinner .... **Pages 81–82**

- Try It Out: Page 82
  1. (c)
  2. Answers will vary.
  3. Answers will vary.
  4. (b)

Assessment Answers

Making Inferences .... **Page 86**

1. (d)
2. Poseidon was the god of the sea and considered to be a very important god.
3. Yes; Answers should include they built tunnels, harbors, temples, magnificent palaces, huge stone wall, etc.
4. Rich; Answers should indicate that people would have to be rich to afford a magnificent palace in the mountains with a beautiful view.

DRAWING CONCLUSIONS

- Make sure you understand what it is you are drawing conclusions about.
- Look in the text to find the facts and details.
- Make decisions about what they mean.
- Always check all possible answers before deciding on your answer.

SUMMARIZING

- Check the text to be sure you understand the question. Then, find the keywords.
- Find information in the text that is most important to your understanding of it. Decide how it is connected.
- Take out any unnecessary details or unconnected information.
- Always check all possible answers before deciding on your answer.

MAKING INFERENCES

- The answers are usually not in the text, but there is information that will give you clues to think about.
- Find the answer that makes the most sense and is supported by the text.
- Always consider all possible answers before making a decision.

Drawing Conclusions

Name _____

When you draw conclusions, you are making a decision or judgment after considering all the information. We draw conclusions about what we read by finding facts and details in the text, taking it all into consideration, and then making judgments about it.

Activity: Read the passage below and complete pages 66–68.

Guide Dogs

1.   Do you know how a dog is chosen and trained to be a guide dog?

2.   A guide dog is trained to help blind or visually impaired people get around at home and in public. It is allowed to go with its owner into shops, restaurants, hotels, buses, trains, planes—in fact, anywhere its owner wants to go.

3.   Labrador retrievers are most commonly used as guide dogs. Other breeds include golden retrievers and German shepherds. Many of these breeds have the qualities needed to be a guide dog. These include intelligence, obedience, friendliness, willingness to learn, ability to concentrate for a long time, calmness, and a good memory.

4.   When a puppy that is thought to be suitable to be trained as a guide dog is ready to leave its mother, it is given to a volunteer puppy raiser. This person, or family, will have been carefully chosen by a guide dog school. The puppy raiser will keep the dog and teach it the basics of being a guide dog before it is ready to be properly trained.

5.   Puppy raisers teach the dog how to sit, lie down, stay, and walk correctly on a leash. They train the puppy using lots of praise and never give food rewards. This is so it can work around food and not be distracted from its job. They make sure the puppy is given all kinds of experiences. These include feeling comfortable in noisy, crowded places; hearing sudden, loud noises; being in bad weather outdoors; being near traffic; going around objects; and not being distracted by other animals.

6.   At about 18 months, a suitable dog leaves the puppy raiser and learns more difficult skills from a special trainer for three or four months. It learns to walk just ahead and to the left of the trainer and how to stop at curbs, cross the road, handle itself safely around traffic, stop at stairs, go around objects, spot possible dangers, and most of all, not to be distracted. It is important that people in the street do not come up and pet a guide dog in its working harness.

7.   Finally, it is ready to learn to work with its new visually impaired master. This takes about a month. A guide dog seems to have a hard job, but it loves its work and only wants love and affection as a reward.

Name _____

Follow the steps below to learn how to draw conclusions.

- Conclusions are decisions you make after careful consideration of facts and details in the text.
- Find out what you are making conclusions about.
- Look in the text to find the facts and details. Underline them.
- Make decisions about what they mean.
- Check all answers before choosing one.

1. Why are some dogs trained to be guide dogs?
   (a) Guide dogs make good pets.
   (b) Guide dogs can go on trains.
   (c) Guide dogs love their work.
   (d) Guide dogs help blind or visually impaired people.

2. Choose the best answer. Think about each choice carefully.
   (a) Guide dogs might make good pets, but it doesn't explain why they are trained. This is not the right answer.
   (b) The text says guide dogs are allowed on trains, but it doesn't explain why they are trained. This is not the right answer.
   (c) The text says guide dogs love their work, but it doesn't explain why they are trained. This is not the right answer.
   (d) The text says a guide dog is trained for this reason. This is the right answer.

1. Why does a puppy raiser need to be carefully chosen?
   (a) Puppy raisers are paid a lot of money.
   (b) Puppy raisers need to be people who like dogs.
   (c) Puppy raisers need to be the kind of people who will teach a young dog important things.
   (d) Puppy raisers give the puppy different experiences.

2. Choose the best answer. Think about each choice carefully.
   (a) The text says puppy raisers are volunteers, which means they do their job for free. This is not the right answer.
   (b) Puppy raisers would have to like dogs, but this does not explain why they are carefully chosen. This is not the right answer.
   (c) The text says that puppy raisers keep the dog and teach it the basics of being a good guide dog. It is very important that they do this. This seems to be the best answer so far. Remember, you must check all the answers.
   (d) The text says that puppy raisers give the puppy all kinds of experiences, but it doesn't explain why they are carefully chosen. This is not the right answer.

Drawing Conclusions

Name _____

Use the strategies you learned to practice drawing conclusions. Use the clues in the "Think!" boxes to help you.

1. You can conclude that guide dogs would be allowed in taxis because:
   - (a) the text says they are allowed on trains.
   - (b) they like riding in taxis.
   - (c) the text says a guide dog can go anywhere its owner wants to go.
   - (d) they are properly trained and would behave in a taxi.

> **Think!**
> You will need to read paragraph 2 to find the answer.

2. Which word would **not** describe a guide dog?
   - (a) nervous
   - (b) intelligent
   - (c) obedient
   - (d) patient

> **Think!**
> You will need to read paragraph 3 and think about what each word means in the last sentence to find the answer.

3. Which tells you that you would most likely see a Labrador retriever as someone's guide dog?
   - (a) People like Labrador retrievers.
   - (b) They are friendly and intelligent.
   - (c) Labrador retrievers like stopping at curbs.
   - (d) They are the most commonly used guide dog.

> **Think!**
> Read paragraph 3 to find the answer.

4. You can conclude that a guide dog would not be frightened if it heard thunder because . . .

   _____

   _____

   _____

   _____

> **Think!**
> You will need to read paragraph 5 and think about all the things a guide dog must get used to.

Name _____

Use the strategies you have been practicing to help you draw conclusions.

1. If a dog is chosen to go to a special trainer to learn more and become a guide dog, you could conclude that:

    (a)   it was a friendly dog.

    (b)   it wasn't easily distracted by noise, crowds, or other animals.

    (c)   the puppy raiser loved it.

    (d)   the puppy raiser had trouble training it.

2. What can you conclude to be the reason a guide dog is not given food as a training reward?

    (a)   Guide dogs prefer to find their own food.

    (b)   Guide dogs only like praise as a reward.

    (c)   Food is too expensive to give as a reward.

    (d)   If food is given as a reward, the guide dog might forget about the job.

3. About how long does a guide dog take to be fully trained?

    (a)   two years

    (b)   one year

    (c)   eighteen months

    (d)   four months

4. Explain how you chose your answer to question 3.

    _____

    _____

    _____

    _____

Drawing Conclusions

Name _____

Activity: Read the letter below and complete page 70.

Ban Cats!

Dear Mr. Mayor,

1.   Many people are concerned about cats roaming around outside, especially at night. I think that cats should be banned from being outside and kept inside at night.

2.   It's bad enough that cats are free to roam around freely during the day. They simply jump up and over the fence and begin to poke their noses into someone else's backyard without even being invited. People don't do that, and dogs have to be kept in their own backyard. Why should cats be able to do this?

3.   The problem is worse at night. During the day, you can usually see what a cat is up to and shoo it away. At night, it is dark and you are in bed, hopefully asleep. A cat can come into your yard and dig to do its "business" in your garden. Then, you get up in the morning and have to clean it up.

4.   Cats save their fighting with other cats until night—or they seem to. You can be sound asleep having a pleasant dream, when it is interrupted by a terrible wailing noise followed by high-pitched screeches. It's the neighborhood cats that are allowed out at night having a meeting to see who can wake up the most neighbors! They choose other people's roofs and walls to do this on—not their own! And it goes on ALL night.

5.   When it begins to get light, cats that are out at night are able to do something that really upsets me—stalk innocent birds! You wake up to hear birds making their morning singsong in the trees, and cats are creeping up on them to catch them. Although some owners put bells on their cats, they don't always warn a bird the cat is nearby.

6.   It really is time that cat owners are forced to keep their cats inside at night. Don't you agree?

Sincerely,
Mark

Try It Out

Name _____

Use the strategies you learned and practiced in *Guide Dogs* to help you practice drawing conclusions.

Remember:

- Conclusions are decisions you make about the meaning of facts and details in the text.
- Find what you are drawing conclusions about.
- Look in the text to find the facts and details. Underline them.
- Make decisions about what they mean.
- Check all answers before deciding.

1. What do you think the writer wants to happen?

   (a)   cats to be banned

   (b)   cats to be kept inside at night

   (c)   people to be banned from owning cats

   (d)   people to be made to put bells on their cats

   Think!

   Read paragraph 6.

2. Explain the main reason the writer sometimes gets woken up at night.

   _____

   _____

   _____

3. What cat behavior bothers the writer the most?

   (a)   Cats fighting at night.   (b)   Cats going to the bathroom in the garden.

   (c)   Cats preying on birds.   (d)   Cats not wearing bells.

4. Do you think the writer:

   (a) hates cats, or

   (b) just wants them banned from being outside at night?

   Explain why you chose your answer.

   _____

   _____

Summarizing

Name _____

Summarizing is giving the main ideas or facts without using many words. We need to link the important ideas and decide which are the main points.

Activity: Read the passage below and complete pages 72–74.

Seahorses

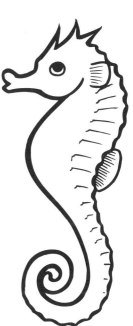

1.   Seahorses are a type of small fish. They are very unusual-looking, which makes some people think they are not real and are even a myth like mermaids.

2.   Seahorses get their name from the shape of their head, which is long and horse-shaped. They have a curved tail and range in size from 0.6 in. to 14 in. Seahorses vary in color—white, yellow, black, brown, and gray, and some are banded or even spotted. Instead of scales like most fish, seahorses have a hard outer covering like a crab, with little spines like a puffer fish. Their eyes move independently like a lizard, so they can look forwards and backwards at the same time. Seahorses have a snout like an aardvark and no teeth.

3.   They are found all over the world in the warm water of reefs, in seaweed beds, and also in freshwater habitats. Seahorses are not very good swimmers and move very slowly, mostly up and down with their heads up and their tails down. They use their monkey-like tail like a hand to hold on to sea plants to prevent them from being swept away by the current while they look for food. Seahorses use their snout like a straw to eat their food, which includes krill, small shrimp, and other tiny crustaceans.

4.   Seahorses can change color very quickly, like a chameleon, and blend in with their surroundings. This is called *camouflage.* It is a very effective way of protecting themselves from their enemies.

5.   Female seahorses produce eggs, but they deposit them into a male's kangaroo-like "pouch." The males keep them in their pouch for about 40–50 days until they hatch. They give birth to about 100 sea ponies that are less than 1 cm in length. The sea ponies must now look after themselves. Seahorses can live for about four years.

6.   Seahorses are mainly endangered by water pollution because they live close to the coast or in polluted waterways. Huge numbers are collected to be used for aquarium pets in some countries. In other countries, they are also dried and sold as souvenirs or used in traditional medicine to treat such things as asthma and skin diseases.

Name _____

Follow the steps below to learn how to determine the main points and summarize text.

- Make sure you understand the question. Underline the keywords.
- Look for information in the text. Decide what is important and how it is connected.
- Leave out any information you don't need.
- Check all the answers before making a decision.

1. Which sentence best summarizes how and what a seahorse eats?

(a) Seahorses eat krill, shrimp, and other tiny crustaceans they find in the water.

(b) Seahorses are not good swimmers, and they hold on to plants while they search for food.

(c) Seahorses have a monkey-like tail, which they use to hold on to plants while they look for food.

(d) Seahorses use their tail to hold on to plants while they eat small crustaceans with their snout.

2. Choose the best answer. Think about each choice carefully.

(a) This sentence tells what seahorses eat, but it doesn't tell about how they eat. It is not a good answer.

(b) The fact that seahorses do not swim well and need to hold on to plants does not summarize how and what they eat. This is not a good answer.

(c) This sentence tells how seahorses search for food, but it doesn't tell what they eat. It is not the best answer.

(d) This sentence summarizes how they eat—using their tail and their snout—and what they eat. This is the best answer.

1. Which sentence would you leave out of a summary of how seahorses reproduce?

(a) Female seahorses deposit eggs into the male's pouch.

(b) Seahorses live for about four years.

(c) The eggs are kept in the male's pouch for about 40–50 days.

(d) Males give birth to about 100 sea ponies.

2. Choose the best answer. Think about each choice carefully.

(a) This is an important point about reproduction and needs to be in the summary.

(b) This is interesting, but it doesn't tell about reproducing. It seems to be the answer, but all answers need to be checked before making a decision.

(c) This is an important point and is about reproduction. It needs to be in the summary.

(d) This is another important point about reproduction and needs to be in the summary.

Summarizing

Name _____

Use the strategies you learned to practice summarizing. Use the clues in the "Think!" boxes to help you.

1. Which is the best summary of the type of information about seahorses in paragraph 2?

    (a) how seahorses reproduce

    (b) where seahorses are found

    (c) what seahorses eat

    (d) what seahorses look like

> **Think!**
> You will need to read paragraph 2 before deciding.

2. List three points to summarize where seahorses might be found.

    • _____

    • _____

    • _____

> **Think!**
> Read paragraph 3 carefully to find the answer, and leave out any words that aren't needed.

3. What sentence best summarizes all the important points of paragraph 1?

    (a) Seahorses are unusual-looking fish that some people think are a myth.

    (b) Seahorses are a type of small fish.

    (c) Seahorses are a myth like mermaids.

    (d) Seahorses are an unusual fish and are real.

> **Think!**
> Read paragraph 1 and underline the important points.

4. Write a short sentence to summarize how seahorses swim.

    _____

    _____

    _____

> **Think!**
> Read paragraph 3 and underline the important points about how they swim.

Name _____

Use the strategies you have been practicing to help you summarize.

1. Write keywords to summarize what each part of a seahorse looks like.

(a)	head	
(b)	snout	
(c)	tail	
(d)	covering	
(e)	color	

2. Which sentence best summarizes the information about seahorses in paragraph 4?
   (a) Seahorses can protect themselves from their enemies.
   (b) Seahorses can change color.
   (c) Seahorses use camouflage to protect themselves from their enemies.
   (d) Seahorses blend in with their surroundings.

3. Write a sentence to summarize how a seahorse uses its tail when eating.

   _____

   _____

   _____

4. Write a short summary to explain why seahorses are endangered.

   _____

   _____

   _____

Name _____

Activity: Read the poem below and complete page 76.

One of Those Days

1.   Had one of those days.
        You know what I mean.
        When everything you do
        makes you feel blue!

2.   Crawled out of bed late.
        Forgot to set my alarm.
        Which made Mom mad,
        and that was bad!

3.   Burned my toast.
        Found an empty jar of jam.
        When I spilled juice on the floor,
        Mom sent me packing out the door!

4.   Bike had a flat tire.
        Had to run to school.
        Left my homework on my bed.
        You can guess what my teacher said!

5.   Found soggy sandwiches.
        My drink had leaked.
        Teacher caught me talking in school.
        I should know the rule!

6.   Had a fight with my brother.
        Mom sent us to our room.
        No dessert for us tonight.
        It just isn't right!

7.   At last the day is over.
        Time for sleep.
        But the noise that I can hear
        Is my brother snoring in my ear!

Try It Out

Name _____

Use the strategies you learned and practiced in *Seahorses* to help you summarize information.

> **Remember:**
> - Make sure you understand the question. Underline the keywords.
> - Look for information in the text. Decide what is important and how it is connected.
> - Leave out any information you don't need.
> - Check all possible answers before making a decision.

1. Which sentence best summarizes what happened to the writer and his brother?

   (a) They had a fight, and Mom punished them.

   (b) Mom sent them to their room.

   (c) They couldn't have any dessert.

   (d) The boys had a fight.

   Think!
   Read stanza 6.

2. Summarize the three things the poet did that his mom was upset with him about.

   _____

   _____

   _____

3. Summarize the two things the poet did that his teacher was upset with him about.

   _____

   _____

4. The poet had five bad things happen to him related to food or drink. Write a summary of these.

   _____

   _____

   _____

   _____

Making Inferences

Name _____

When we read, we often decide what we think might be true based on information in the text. This is called *making inferences*.

Activity: Read the story below and complete pages 78–80.

The Story of King Midas

1.   King Midas was a very rich king who ruled the kingdom of Phygia. He lived in a huge castle with his lovely, fair-haired daughter, Marigold. His castle was filled with beautiful and expensive things. It was surrounded by magnificent flower gardens, the biggest being one filled with sweet-smelling roses.

2.   Midas also enjoyed collecting gold. Every day, he would count his huge pile of gold again and again. If his daughter picked a bunch of dandelions or buttercups, he would say that he wished the flowers were as golden as they looked. Then they would really be worth keeping.

3.   One day, while Midas was outside in his rose garden counting his coins, he saw an old man resting behind a bush. He realized the man was Silenus, the faithful servant of the god Dionysus. Midas thought it would be a good idea if he looked after him, so he took extra special care of him for a week before taking him back to Dionysus. Of course, Dionysus rewarded Midas for his kindness by granting him one wish. Midas thought for just one second and wished that everything he touched would turn to gold. Dionysus frowned and asked if he was sure. When Midas replied that he was sure, Dionysus finally agreed.

4.   Midas ran around the castle touching the walls, the furniture, and his precious roses. They all turned to gold. Then, he sat down and began to eat a meal but found he couldn't eat it, as it had turned to gold as well. Suddenly, Marigold ran into the room. She grabbed her father's arm, saying that his roses had turned an ugly yellow color and didn't smell sweet anymore. Midas began to tell her what he thought about them, but to his horror, she too had turned into gold.

5.   Midas was so upset that he went back to Dionysus and begged him to get rid of his golden touch. He said he was sorry he had made such a wish. Dionysus looked at him carefully and then agreed. He told him to bathe in the river water to wash off his greed and the wish. Midas gladly did this and then collected water in jugs to pour over everything that had turned to gold.

6.   From that day on, the only thing Midas enjoyed that was golden was his daughter's hair.

Name _____

Follow the steps below to learn how to determine what is most likely to be true.

> - The answers are not usually in the text, but there is information to give you clues to think about. (This could be underlined.)
> - Find the answer that makes the most sense and is supported by details from the text.
> - Consider all possible answers before making a decision.

1. What is the best reason why King Midas's daughter was named Marigold?

   (a) She was named after her mother, who was called Marigold.

   (b) Midas liked flowers, and a marigold is a flower.

   (c) Her name starts with M and Midas starts with M.

   (d) Midas loved gold, and the word *gold* is part of her name.

2. Choose the best answer. Think about each choice carefully.

   (a) The text doesn't say that her mother's name was Marigold. This is not the best answer.

   (b) This is a possible answer as the sentence is true, but you must check all possible answers.

   (c) There is nothing in the text to make you think this sentence is the reason, but it could be. It may not be the best answer.

   (d) The text says how much Midas likes gold and counts it again and again. He probably wanted the word *gold* in his daughter's name. This would be a better answer than (b) or (c).

1. Which flowers do you think Midas liked best?

   (a) marigolds

   (b) roses

   (c) buttercups

   (d) dandelions

2. Choose the best answer. Think about each choice carefully.

   (a) His daughter's name was Marigold, but the text doesn't say anything about marigold flowers. It could be a good answer.

   (b) The text says the biggest garden was his rose garden and that Midas counted his money in his precious rose garden and that he turned his precious roses into gold. This is a better answer than (a).

   (c) Buttercups are a gold color, but Midas said they would be only worth keeping if they were golden. They may not be his favorite flowers.

   (d) Midas also said that dandelions would not be worth keeping unless they were golden. This is not a good answer.

Making Inferences

Name _____

Use the strategies you learned to help you determine what is most likely to be true based on information from the text. Use the clues in the "Think!" boxes to help you.

1. Why do you think Midas took extra special care of Silenus for a week?

   (a) Because Silenus was tired and had nowhere to sleep.

   (b) Because he was the god Dionysus's servant.

   (c) Midas liked having visitors.

   (d) He had a feeling Dionysus would reward him.

> **Think!**
> Read paragraph 3 carefully to help you decide on the answer.

2. How did Midas feel when he was first granted his wish?

   (a) the same

   (b) upset

   (c) overjoyed

   (d) worried

> **Think!**
> You will need to read the beginning of paragraph 4 to find the answer.

3. What information from the text helped you answer question 2?

   _____

   _____

4. Do you think Midas was a deep and thoughtful thinker?

   Yes ◯   No ◯

   Explain why you decided to choose this answer.

   _____

   _____

> **Think!**
> The best clue to help you is in paragraph 3.

5. Explain how you think Marigold felt when she discovered the roses had turned to gold.

   _____

   _____

   _____

> **Think!**
> Read paragraph 4 to help you decide the answer.

Name _____

Use the strategies you have been practicing to help you make inferences.

1. Most likely, how did Midas first feel about his roses turning to gold?
   (a) He liked them better the way they were before.
   (b) He liked their smell.
   (c) He was pleased they were gold.
   (d) He was sad they were gold.

2. Dionysus looked carefully at Midas before agreeing to get rid of his golden touch. What would be the best reason why he did this?
   (a) He thought Midas looked funny.
   (b) He wanted to be sure Midas was certain.
   (c) He had to look carefully because he didn't have his glasses on.
   (d) He was looking to see if Midas had turned to gold.

3. Give a reason to explain why Dionysus frowned when Midas first asked for his wish.

   _____

   _____

   _____

   _____

4. Do you think that Midas eventually loved his daughter more than gold?

   Yes ◯   No ◯

   Explain why you think this.

   _____

   _____

   _____

   _____

Name _____

Activity: Read the story below and complete page 82.

Surprise Dinner

1. Last weekend, our family went to Jackson Lake, where we have a vacation house. In the shed is the small dinghy my older brother and I are allowed to use on the lake.

2. Right after breakfast on Saturday, Jordan and I raced over to the shed and yanked open the door to get the dinghy out. We put on two life jackets and packed the oars, anchor, fishing line, two buckets, a net, cutting knife, and board. Then, we dragged the dinghy down the driveway, across the lawn, and down the track to the shore. Our younger brother, Daniel, stood at the top of the track, sadly watching us climbing into the boat.

3. I took the first turn to row towards our fishing spot. Jordan thinks I row quite well—for a girl! After a while, Jordan had a turn. He can row faster than I can, so we soon reached our spot. When we were setting up for fishing, we realized we had forgotten to bring the bait. Jordan angrily grabbed the oars and began to row back towards the shore.

4. He was so mad that he wouldn't give me a turn, and he wasn't very careful about where he was going. I yelled out to him that he was heading towards the sandbank, but it was too late. The dinghy hit the sandbank, rocking the boat and making us lose our balance. We had to grip the sides of the dinghy so we wouldn't fall out. I watched in horror as the oars flew off the side of the boat and landed in the water.

5. I grabbed a bucket and began to use it as an oar to try to reach the real oars before they drifted away. Jordan grabbed the other bucket and did the same. He managed to reach out and pluck the oars out of the water just in time.

6. Suddenly, I heard a splashing noise coming from the bucket I was still holding. We looked inside the bucket and couldn't believe our eyes. To our surprise, I had caught a trout. We hadn't needed that bait after all!

Name _____

Use the strategies you learned and practiced in *The Story of King Midas* to help you determine what is most likely true.

> **Remember:**
> - The answers are not usually in the text, but there is information to give you clues to think about. (This could be underlined.)
> - Find the answer that makes the most sense and is supported by details from the text.
> - Consider all possible answers before making a decision.

1. What would be the best reason why Daniel sadly watched his brother and sister climb into the boat?
   (a)   He had hurt himself.
   (b)   He knew what was going to happen.
   (c)   He wasn't allowed to go.
   (d)   He had got into trouble.

> **Think!**
> Read paragraphs 1 and 2 to help you decide which answer to choose.

2. I think the writer chose the title *Surprise Dinner* because . . .

   _____

   _____

3. Do you think Jordan and his sister had to drag the dinghy very far to the shore?

   Yes ◯   No ◯

   Explain why you decided to choose this answer.

   _____

   _____

4. Most likely, what kind of board did Jordan and his sister take on the dinghy?
   (a)   boogie board
   (b)   cutting board
   (c)   surfboard
   (d)   skateboard

Name _____

Activity: Read the story below, and use pages 84–86 to show how well you can draw conclusions, summarize, and make inferences.

The Lost City of Atlantis

1. Long ago, there was an island called Atlantis. It was in the middle of the Atlantic Ocean.

2. Atlantis was ruled by King Atlas, the oldest son of Poseidon, god of the sea. It was a beautiful island, with mountains, lakes, forests, animals, waterfalls, rivers, and green fields. The capital city was built on top of a hill surrounded by rings of water. The rings were joined by tunnels so ships could sail through from the ocean. Many people worked on the harbor docks, loading and unloading cargo. In the very center of the hill, a huge temple was built to the god of the sea. Inside, it had a gold statue of Poseidon driving six winged horses. The temple was made from the most precious metals.

3. In the green fields not far from the city lived the farmers, who grew delicious fruits, vegetables, and some herbs and nuts for the people of Atlantis. In the mountains looking over these fields and the ocean, people lived in magnificent palaces. Atlantis also had a great army of thousands of men. The city was built behind a huge stone wall.

4. For a long time, the people of Atlantis led simple lives and were good, kind people. But gradually, they became greedier and greedier and wanted power over everything. Zeus, the god of sky and thunder, saw this and became angry. He gathered all the gods, and together they created great explosions that violently shook the island. Atlantis collapsed into the ocean and was never seen again.

5. The legend of Atlantis is one of the oldest in the world. Most people think that Atlantis never existed. Those who do believe it existed wonder what really caused its destruction. Some people still search under the sea to see if they can find the lost city.

Name _____

Remember:

- What is it you are drawing conclusions about?
- Look in the text to find the facts and details. Underline them.
- Make decisions about what they mean.
- Check all answers before deciding.

---

1. You can conclude that Atlantis got its name because:
   (a) the ruler, King Atlas, liked the name.
   (b) it was named after the ocean.
   (c) Poseidon chose the name.
   (d) Zeus chose the name.

2. Why did Zeus conclude that Atlantis should be destroyed?
   (a) There wasn't enough food there.
   (b) The people were unhappy.
   (c) He was angry with the people.
   (d) He was a grumpy god.

3. Would you conclude that Atlantis was a safe place to live?

   Yes ⭕   No ⭕

   Explain why you chose this answer.

   _____

   _____

   _____

4. What can you tell about the diet of the people of Atlantis?

   _____

   _____

   _____

   _____

Summarizing

Name _____

Remember:

- Make sure you understand the question. Underline the keywords.
- Look for information in the text. Decide what is important and how it is connected.
- Leave out any information you don't need.
- Check all the answers before making a decision.

1. Which sentence best summarizes what people did in Atlantis?
   (a) They lived in a beautiful place with mountains, lakes, rivers, and green fields.
   (b) They built a huge temple in the center of the hill.
   (c) They enjoyed a simple life on a very beautiful island.
   (d) They had a great time.

2. Which sentence best summarizes how Atlantis was protected?
   (a) Atlantis had a huge army to protect it.
   (b) The people of Atlantis protected their property because they were rich.
   (c) The gods Zeus and Poseidon protected Atlantis.
   (d) Atlantis had a huge wall surrounding it and a great army to protect it.

3. Write a sentence to describe Poseidon's temple. Include the most important information.

   _____

   _____

   _____

4. Write a short summary about why Atlantis was destroyed.

   _____

   _____

   _____

   _____

Name _____

> **Remember:**
>
> - The answers are not usually in the text, but there is information to give you clues to think about. (This could be underlined.)
> - Find the answer that makes the most sense and is supported by details from the text.
> - Consider all possible answers before making a decision.

1. Zeus and the other gods created great explosions that violently shook the island and made it collapse and sink into the ocean. What could those explosions most likely have been?

    (a)   a very loud thunderstorm

    (b)   waves crashing

    (c)   a tornado

    (d)   a volcano erupting

2. Why do you think Poseidon's temple was built of the most precious metals that could be found?

    _____

    _____

    _____

3. Do you think the people of Atlantis were good builders? Explain why you think this.

    Yes ◯   No ◯

    _____

    _____

    _____

4. What kind of people do you think lived in the mountains? Give a reason for your answer.

    Rich ◯   Poor ◯

    _____

    _____

Cause and Effect

Lesson Objective

- Students will determine cause and effect and understand how they are connected.

Background Information

Students need to understand that a cause leads to an effect and that they are connected.

This section demonstrates strategies for students to use in order to find information in a text, which in turn helps them to make the connection to determine cause and effect.

They need to find and underline the keywords in questions, and then search for information in the text that makes connections between the keywords and either the cause or the effect. They need to understand that they will be given either a cause or an effect in the question, but they will need to search for the other.

Activity Answers

Beach Safety .... Pages 91–94

- Practice Page: Page 93
  1. (c)
  2. (a)
  3. The driver may not be able to see and avoid the swimmer; they travel very quickly
  4. It can lead to skin cancer and damage to the eyes.
- On Your Own: Page 94
  1. (b)
  2. (b)
  3. You can prevent this effect by wearing a hat, T-shirt, sunglasses, and sunscreen.
  4. Answers will vary.

Floating Liquids .... Pages 95–96

- Try It Out: Page 96
  1. (d)
  2. The oil is the lightest or the least dense, so it will float on top of the others.
  3. If you don't add food coloring, the water won't be clearly seen.
  4. (c) The marble will sink to the bottom because it is a heavy object. Answers may vary.

Assessment Answers

Cause and Effect .... Page 110

  1. (d)
  2. The mask drops down if more oxygen is needed in the plane.
  3. Mom helped the kids pack a backpack of things to do.
  4. (b)

Lesson Objective

- Students will demonstrate their ability to identify facts and opinions and their understanding of how they differ.

Background Information

A fact is something that is true. It can be verified by referring to other information. In other words, it can be checked and be proven to be correct.

An opinion is something that someone believes to be true but cannot be verified. In other words, it is something that someone *thinks* rather than knows is true.

Students must be able to distinguish between facts and opinions in order to become critical readers. They have to engage and interact with text and read with a questioning attitude. They can then look for relationships and critically judge and evaluate what they read by identifying facts and opinions.

Critical readers become more discriminating consumers of the news media and advertising—an important life skill.

Activity Answers

A Plant That Eats Insects..**Pages 97–100**

- Practice Page: Page 99
  1. (a)
  2. (d)
  3. All that is left of the insect is the hard, outer part.
  4. Answers will vary.
- On Your Own: Page 100
  1. (b)
  2. (a) A Plant That Eats Insects
     (b) It is a fact. The passage talks about the Venus flytrap and how it eats insects.
  3. Two facts: The plant opens up in about 12 hours. The plant "spits" out the object.
  4. Everyone is very interested to know how the trap actually shuts.
  5. Answers will vary.

The Country Life Is For Me! ....**Pages 101–102**

- Try It Out: Page 102
  1. (d)
  2. (a)
  3. Fact: There are more shops in the city. Opinion: You can waste your money in the city shops.
  4. Answers will vary.

Assessment Answers

Fact or Opinion .... **Page 111**

1. (a)
2. (d)
3. Fact: The taxi ride to the airport took 45 minutes.
   Opinion: The taxi ride to the airport seemed like ages.
4. Dad thought it was nothing compared to how long the rest of the trip would take.

Point of View and Purpose

Unit 4

Lesson Notes

Lesson Objective

- Students will understand and identify the writer's point of view and purpose.

Background Information

The writer's point of view is his or her opinion about a subject. A reader should, after careful and detailed analysis of what has been written, understand and be able to identify the point of view expressed in the text.

The writer's purpose for writing explains why the text was written. It may be to express a particular point of view, to amuse, entertain, inform, persuade, instruct, describe, record information, or to explain something.

Students should be encouraged to try to determine how and what the writer was thinking and use this to help them make decisions about the writer's point of view. They should then look for details in the text to support or reject the choices they have made. (These can be underlined.)

All possible choices should be considered before a final decision is made.

Activity Answers

Request for a Bike Track .... Pages 103–106

- Practice Page: Page 105
  1. (b)
  2. (a) The corner of Scott Avenue and Wade Road
     (b) Answers could include: it has a large area of vacant land, has an area suitable for a track as well as sitting and playing areas, has a sandy area suitable for curving and grading to make a track
  3. It is easy to go too fast and have an accident.
  4. Answers will vary.
- On Your Own: Page 106
  1. (c)
  2. There are too many children to ride in the driveways, which means they can bang into smaller children and each other, and scrape parked cars.
  3. She thinks parents and children could hold fundraising activities to help pay for the bike track.
  4. Answers will vary.

Double Trouble ....Pages 107–108

- Try It Out: Page 108
  1. (c)
  2. The writer thinks the twins' rhyming names are confusing, and he or she gets their names muddled.
  3. (b)
  4. Answers will vary.

Assessment Answers

Point of View and Purpose .... Page 112
  1. (c)
  2. (b)
  3. Answers will vary.
  4. Answers will vary.

Helpful Hints

CAUSE AND EFFECT

- A cause (what happened first) leads to an effect (what happened as a result of the cause). They are connected.

- You are given either a cause or an effect, and you will need to find the other.

- Look for keywords in the question. Then, find the words in the text that are connected to the keywords.

- Check all possible answers before making a decision.

FACT OR OPINION

- A fact is something that can be checked and proven to be correct.

- An opinion is what someone believes to be true, but it can't be proven. Read the text to decide what can be proven (fact) by the text.

- Always check all possible answers before deciding on your answer.

POINT OF VIEW AND PURPOSE

- Writers do not always tell you what they believe. You may have to come to this conclusion based on the information you have read.

- Look for details and information in the text to help you decide why the author may have written the text or what the author's point of view is.

- Always check all possible answers before deciding on your answer.

Cause and Effect

Name _____

Cause and effect is a phrase we use to explain when one thing (a cause) makes something else happen (an effect). If you want to understand what you read, you must be able to determine the cause(s) and the effect(s) in the text.

Activity: Read the passage below and complete pages 92–94.

Beach Safety

1.   Playing in and around water can be fun. However, there are things you should do to stay safe. Most water safety rules apply no matter where you are. These are some important things I learned about staying safe at beaches.

2.   If you are swimming or playing near a jetty, always know how deep the water is before jumping or diving in. The water can be shallower than you think, and neck and back injuries can occur. Look carefully when walking along the water's edge, as hidden logs, rocks, or broken glass can bruise or cut your feet. Also, enter the water slowly if it is cold. You can feel as if you are losing your breath and panic if you enter cold water too fast. You won't be able to float or swim properly.

3.   Read and obey signs that give rules to swimmers. An important one to obey is not to swim near a boat ramp, waterskiers, or jet skis. It is difficult for the drivers of these vehicles to see and avoid swimmers, who can be seriously hurt.

4.   When you are at the beach, swim in the designated areas marked off by lifeguards. The water between the markers is generally calmer, and there will not be rip tides. Rip tides are large bodies of water that move back out to sea. If you do get caught in a rip, don't try to fight it and swim back to shore. It's too strong. The current right under the water is very strong, and you will feel as if you are being pulled under. Try to float on top while the rip is taking you out to sea. Swim parallel to the shore and put your hand up to signal for help. Lifeguards can put you into their rescue boat. Always swim in view of a lifeguard at the beach or public pool so they can help you, if necessary.

5.   If you are climbing on rocks near the shore or walking on a reef at low tide, it is a good idea to wear footwear. This will protect your feet from cuts or stings from sea creatures, such as a stingray.

6.   Finally, keep your skin safe when in and around water. Wear a hat, a T-shirt, sunscreen, and sunglasses to protect your skin and eyes from the glare and harmful rays of the sun. Sun exposure over a long period of time can cause skin cancer and damage your eyes.

Name _____

Follow the steps below to learn how you can identify the cause and effect.

- A cause leads to an effect, and they are connected.
- You will be told one, and you will need to identify the other.
- Look for keywords in the question and underline them.
- Find words in the text that are connected to keywords in the question.
- Check all answers before deciding.

1. If you don't check how deep the water is before jumping or diving in, you could:
   - (a) feel cold.
   - (b) cut your foot.
   - (c) wave your arms.
   - (d) hurt your neck or back.

2. Choose the best answer. Think about each choice carefully.
   - (a) You could feel cold, but it isn't an effect of not checking the depth of the water. This is not the right answer.
   - (b) Again, this isn't an effect of not checking the depth of the water. This is not the right answer.
   - (c) You could do this, but it is not an effect of not checking the depth of the water. This is not the right answer.
   - (d) The text says neck and back injuries could occur if the water is shallow. This is the best answer.

1. If you swim near a boat ramp:
   - (a) , you might get to go fishing in a boat.
   - (b) , you would hear a lot of noisy cars.
   - (c) , you could be seriously hurt by a boat.
   - (d) , you could be seriously hurt by a rip tide.

2. Choose the best answer. Think about each choice carefully.
   - (a) This would not be a very likely effect of swimming near a boat ramp. This may not be the right answer.
   - (b) You probably could hear some cars, but the text doesn't say that. This is not a good answer.
   - (c) The text says that swimmers can be seriously hurt if swimming near a boat ramp. This seems to be the best answer. Remember, you must check all the answers.
   - (d) This is possible but not likely. It doesn't connect with the question. This is not the right answer.

Cause and Effect

Name _____

Use the strategies you learned to practice identifying cause and effect. Use the clues in the "Think!" boxes to help you.

1. What is one effect of entering the water too fast if it is cold?

   (a) You can hurt your back.

   (b) You can be caught in a rip tide.

   (c) You can lose your breath and panic.

   (d) You can hurt your neck.

   > **Think!**
   > You will need to look in paragraph 2 and read the effects of cold water.

2. What could be the effect of not looking when you are walking along the water's edge?

   (a) You could bruise or cut your feet on a hidden object.

   (b) You could get lost.

   (c) You could be caught in a rip tide.

   (d) You could bump into a ship.

   > **Think!**
   > You will need to read paragraph 2 to find the answer.

3. Why can a jet ski cause a swimmer to be seriously hurt?

   _____

   _____

   _____

   _____

   > **Think!**
   > Read paragraph 3 to find the answer.

4. What can be the effect of exposing skin to the sun over a long period of time?

   _____

   _____

   _____

   _____

   > **Think!**
   > You will need to read the last paragraph.

Name _____

Use the strategies you have been practicing to help you identify cause and effect.

1. What is one possible effect of not swimming between the designated swimming areas at the beach?

   (a) The water is calmer outside the markers.

   (b) You could get caught in a rip tide.

   (c) The water is deeper outside the flags.

   (d) You could be hit by the lifeguard's rescue boat.

2. What is the cause of cuts or stings on your feet while walking on a reef at low tide?

   (a) Forgetting to wear a hat.

   (b) Not wearing shoes of some kind.

   (c) Not looking where you are going.

   (d) Walking on the reef too long.

3. How can you prevent the effect the sun can have on your skin and eyes when in and around water?

   _____

   _____

   _____

   _____

4. What happens to someone who is caught in a rip tide?

   _____

   _____

   _____

   _____

Cause and Effect

Name _____

Activity: Read the experiments below and complete page 96.

Floating Liquids

Follow these science experiments to discover how different liquids float or sink and how objects float in different liquids.

Experiment 1

What you need:

- large spoon
- maple syrup
- vegetable oil
- large, clear container
- water with food coloring added (so water can be clearly seen)

What to do:

1. Pour syrup carefully into the container.
2. Pour same amount of vegetable oil slowly into the container over the back of a spoon. (Pouring liquids over back of a spoon stops them from mixing.)
3. Do the same with colored water.
4. Wait for liquids to settle into layers.

Results:

The syrup sinks to the bottom, then the water, and the oil stays on top. This happens because some liquids are denser (thicker) than others. Lighter liquids float, and heavier, denser liquids sink.

Experiment 2

What you need:

- container of liquid layers from Experiment 1
- small objects such as a grape, 2 in. piece of flat pasta, cork, marble, eraser, or plastic toy

What to do:

1. Drop different objects gently into container of liquid layers.
2. Observe what happens.

Results:

Some objects float at different levels in the liquids, depending on how light they are. Others will sink to the bottom as they are too heavy.

Name _____

Use the strategies you learned and practiced in *Beach Safety* to help you identify cause and effect.

Remember:

- A cause leads to an effect, and they are connected.
- You will be told one, and you will need to determine the other.
- Look for keywords in the question and underline them.
- Find words in the text that are connected to keywords in the question.
- Check all answers before deciding.

1. What is the effect of pouring the liquids over the back of a spoon?
   (a) It stops you from pouring in too much liquid.
   (b) You can lick the spoon afterwards.
   (c) You can use the spoon to mix the liquids.
   (d) It stops the liquids from mixing.

Think!
Read the "What to do" section in Experiment 1.

2. Explain the cause of the oil being the top layer of liquid.

   _____

   _____

   _____

3. If you don't add food coloring to the water, . . .

   _____

   _____ .

4. What do you think will happen if you put a marble in the liquids?
   (a) It will float on top.   (b) It will get sticky.
   (c) It will sink to the bottom. (d) It will float on the water.

   Explain why you chose this answer.

   _____

   _____

   _____

Fact or Opinion

Name _____

A fact is something that is true. An opinion is something that someone *thinks* is true. When reading, it is important to understand the difference between facts and opinions and to be able to determine which is which.

Activity: Read the passage below and complete pages 98–100.

A Plant That Eats Insects

1.   Plants that eat insects are called *carnivorous plants* (meat eaters). Most plants only get nutrients (food) from the air and the soil. Carnivorous plants do this too, but they also like to eat juicy animals such as flies, caterpillars, crickets, ants, and other bugs. In this way, they get the extra nutrients they need because the plants grow in poor soils.

2.   One of the most interesting carnivorous plants is the Venus flytrap. It is very interesting to read about how it eats. How can a Venus flytrap eat an insect when it doesn't have teeth?

3.   The Venus flytrap has hinged leaves that open and shut. Some people say the leaves look like jaws when they are open, and others think they look like a clam shell. The ends of the leaves have short, stiff hairs on them. Inside the leaves is a sweet-smelling nectar that insects like to drink. They are attracted by the nice smell. The plant waits patiently while the insect moves towards it. When it touches the hairs on the leaves, the leaves snap shut in less than a second, trapping the insect inside. It doesn't close all the way at first, allowing very small insects to escape.

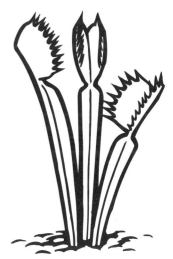

4.   Digestive juices dissolve the soft parts of the insect. About a week later, all that is left of the poor insect is the hard, outer part. The leaves open, and what is left blows away in the wind or washes away in the rain. A pair of flytrap leaves die after about four meals. If an object that isn't food lands in the trap, the plant doesn't like that. It will open up in about 12 hours and "spit" it out!

5.   Everyone is very interested to know just how the trap actually shuts. Scientists still don't know for sure, but they believe it is some kind of pressure on the fluids in the leaves that makes them close.

6.   I think the Venus flytrap is one of the most fascinating plants. I'm glad there aren't giant ones that can eat humans!

Name _____

Follow the steps below to learn how to determine if something is a fact or an opinion.

- Ask yourself:
  Can the statement be checked and proven to be correct? If it can, it is a fact.
  Is it what someone *thinks* is true and can't be proven? If so, it is an opinion.
  For example: Hens lay eggs. (fact)
  Eggs taste good. (opinion)
- Check all possible answers before making a decision.

1. Which sentence gives an opinion?
   (a) Carnivorous plants eat meat.
   (b) Carnivorous plants are found in poor soil.
   (c) Plants get nutrients from the air and soil.
   (d) Carnivorous plants like juicy insects.

2. Choose the best answer. Think about each choice carefully.
   (a) *Carnivorous* means "meat eating." This is a fact that can be checked in a dictionary.
   (b) This information can be proven, so it is a fact.
   (c) Again, this information can be checked and is a fact.
   (d) It is true that carnivorous plants eat insects. However, it is the writer's opinion that they *like* them when they are *juicy*. This is the best answer.

1. Which sentence has both a fact and an opinion?
   (a) The Venus flytrap has leaves that open and shut.
   (b) Insects are attracted to the plant by sweet-smelling nectar.
   (c) The Venus flytrap is the most interesting carnivorous plant.
   (d) The Venus flytrap is a scary plant.

2. Choose the best answer. Think about each choice carefully.
   (a) This sentence has information that can be proven to be a fact. It is not the right answer.
   (b) Again, this sentence has information that can be proven to be a fact. It is not the right answer.
   (c) It is a fact the Venus flytrap is a carnivorous plant. It is the writer's opinion that it is the most interesting. It seems to be the answer, but all answers need to be checked before making a decision.
   (d) This sentence gives only an opinion. It is not the right answer.

Fact or Opinion

Name _____

Use the strategies you learned to practice identifying facts and opinions. Use the clues in the "Think!" boxes to help you.

1. Which sentence is an opinion?

   (a) The plant waits patiently while the insect moves towards it.

   (b) The ends of the leaves have short, stiff hairs.

   (c) The leaves snap shut in less than a second.

   (d) The Venus flytrap eats flies.

> **Think!**
> An opinion is something that someone *believes* is true. Which sentence tells what someone *thinks* is true?

2. Which sentence is a fact?

   (a) The Venus fly trap is interesting to read about.

   (b) The leaves look like jaws.

   (c) The nectar has a nice smell.

   (d) The trap closes when an insect touches the hairs.

> **Think!**
> A fact is something that can be proven to be true. It is not just what someone thinks.

3. Write this sentence from the text as a fact.

   All that is left of the poor insect is the hard, outer part.

   Fact: _____

   _____

   _____

> **Think!**
> What part tells what the writer *thinks* is true? What part gives a fact?

4. Finish this sentence, giving your opinion of the Venus flytrap.

   I think the way the Venus flytrap catches a meal is . . .

   _____

   _____

> **Think!**
> Read the text again and tell what you think.

Name _____

Use the strategies you have been practicing to help you determine if something is a fact or an opinion.

1. Which sentence is an opinion?

    (a) A pair of Venus flytrap leaves die after about four meals.

    (b) The trap looks just like a clam shell.

    (c) The leaves have nectar inside.

    (d) The trap doesn't close all the way at first.

2. (a) Write the title of the passage.

        _____

    (b) Do you think the title is a fact or an opinion? Explain your answer.

        Fact ◯   Opinion ◯

        _____

        _____

3. Read the last two sentences in paragraph 4. Write two facts about what happens if an object that isn't food lands in the trap.

    _____

    _____

    _____

4. Read paragraph 5 and write the opinion in the paragraph.

    Opinion: _____

    _____

5. Read paragraph 3 and write what you think is the most interesting fact.

    Fact: _____

    _____

Name _____

Activity: Read the story below and complete page 102.

The Country Life Is For Me!

1. I think that living in the country is better than living in the city. My family lived for three years in the city, and I was so glad when we moved back to the country.

2. The best thing by far about living in the country is the space and the beautiful, fresh air. In the city, all you can smell is gas fumes from the exhausts of vehicles. Air pollution from transportation and factories in the city can be harmful to your health.

3. The city is a very noisy place. You can hardly hear yourself speak over the noise of vehicle engines running, horns blaring, and brakes squealing. Air-conditioning vents leading out from buildings are also noisy.

4. Everyone in the city is always in a hurry. People rush on their way to work, hurry to do things on their lunch hour, and look unhappy. You hardly ever hear anyone saying "Good morning" or "Good afternoon" or see anyone give you a smile. In the country, people always greet you with a smile and take time to have a chat.

5. There are more traffic lights and busy roads in the city. The traffic is always stop-and-go, with drivers changing lanes, trying to get where they are going a bit quicker. It's dangerous! In the country, the only thing that might stop you is a stray cow on the road.

6. In the city, there are so many adults and children catching trains and buses to work or school; you feel like a sardine squashed up in a tin. In the country, our school bus has plenty of spare seats.

7. There are more shops in the city where you can waste your money on unnecessary things. You can save a lot more by living in the country.

8. Yes, after living in both places, all I can say is that the country life is for me!

Name _____

Use the strategies you learned and practiced in *A Plant That Eats Insects* to help you distinguish between facts and opinions.

Remember:
- Ask yourself:

  Can the statement be checked and proven to be correct? If it can, it is a fact.

  Is it what someone *thinks* is true and can't be proven? If so, it is an opinion.
- Check all the answers before making a decision.

---

1. Which sentence is an opinion?
   - (a) The writer lived for three years in the city.
   - (b) There are more traffic lights in the city.
   - (c) The writer was glad to move back to the country.
   - (d) People look unhappy in the city.

> **Think!**
> An opinion is something that someone *believes* is true. Which sentence tells what someone *thinks* is true?

2. Which sentence is a fact?
   - (a) Air pollution from transportation and factories can be harmful.
   - (b) Everyone in a city is always in a hurry.
   - (c) The city is a very noisy place.
   - (d) People always stop for a chat in the country.

3. Read this sentence and write one fact and one opinion.

   There are more shops in the city where you can waste your money.

   Fact: _____

   _____

   Opinion: _____

   _____

4. Read paragraph 6 and write two opinions.

   Opinion: _____

   _____

   Opinion: _____

   _____

Point of View and Purpose

Name _____

When we read, we should try to think like the writer to figure out how and what he or she feels and believes about the subject (point of view) and why he or she wrote the text (purpose).

Activity: Read the letter below and complete pages 104–106.

Request for a Bike Track

Dear City Council,

1. My name is Janine Miller, and I am the mother of three children, ages six, eight, and ten. I am writing to ask for a bike track to be made in Glenway.

2. There aren't many safe places nearby for my children and their friends to ride their bikes. Our suburb is built on a hill, which means many streets are quite steep. It is too dangerous for them to ride down these streets as it is easy for them to go too fast and have an accident. Riding back up the hills is very hard work, even with gears.

3. Our driveway and neighbors' driveways are not suitable places to ride either. There are too many children on bikes to ride up and down them. I worry about them not only banging into smaller children and each other but also scraping parked cars.

4. Riding along the path around the lake that is over a mile away is also a problem. This path is used by people who want to walk, run, jog, and enjoy the beautiful scenery. It is not a very wide path, and I worry about them keeping out of the way of others, especially parents with strollers.

5. The corner of Scott Avenue and Wade Road would be an ideal place to develop a specially built bike track. This large area of land has a grassy section and some playground equipment at one end. At the other, there are a few trees, some low-lying bushes, and a sandy area. The track could be graded around the trees with curves and bumps. Our children would enjoy riding around safely, while having lots of fun.

6. Having a bike track would have another benefit to the community. Parents could meet and talk to other parents while they watch their children on the track. The children could meet new friends, too. Younger children would enjoy playing on the playground equipment.

7. Fundraising to help pay for the project could be organized by parents and children. Some ideas include bake sales, raffles, and a car wash at the local shopping center.

8. Please think seriously about my request.

Yours sincerely,
Janine Miller

Name _____

Follow the steps below to learn how to identify the writer's point of view and his or her reason for writing the text.

- Writers don't always just tell you what they think or believe or why they have written the text. Sometimes, you have to try to think like they do and come to this conclusion based on what you've read.
- In the text, there are details and information for you to find, underline, and use in choosing the correct answer to each question.
- Consider all possible answers before making a decision.

1. What was Mrs. Miller's main reason for writing the letter?
   - (a) To tell the city council the streets are too steep.
   - (b) To ask the city council for a new driveway.
   - (c) To tell the city council that there aren't enough safe places to ride bikes.
   - (d) To ask the city council to build a bike track.

2. Choose the best answer. Think about each choice carefully.
   - (a) Mrs. Miller does say that the streets are steep, but this doesn't explain why she wrote the letter. This is not the best answer.
   - (b) Mrs. Miller did not say this in her letter. This is not a good answer.
   - (c) Mrs. Miller was concerned about this. It could be the best answer. But you must check all possible answers.
   - (d) Mrs. Miller said this in the first paragraph of her letter. This states the purpose for her letter. It is the best answer.

1. Which of these would Mrs. Miller **not** agree with?
   - (a) Hilly streets aren't safe to ride down.
   - (b) It is hard to ride up steep streets.
   - (c) Driveways are good places to ride.
   - (d) The path around the lake is too narrow for people and bikes.

2. Choose the best answer. Think about each choice carefully.
   - (a) She says and would agree that hilly streets aren't safe to ride down. This is not the right answer.
   - (b) She says and would agree that steep streets are hard to ride up. This is not the right answer.
   - (c) She does not think that driveways are suitable places to ride. This seems to be the best answer.
   - (d) She would agree that this path is too narrow. This is not the right answer.

Point of View and Purpose

Name _____

Use the strategies you learned to practice identifying what the writer believes and why she wrote the text. Use the clues in the "Think!" boxes to help you.

1. Mrs. Miller says that the path around the lake is a problem to ride around. Which of these would she **not** agree with?

   (a) The lake path has a beautiful view.

   (b) The path is wide enough for everyone to use at the same time.

   (c) Many people walk, jog, run, or ride around the path.

   (d) The lake is a popular place to visit.

   > **Think!**
   > Read paragraph 4 carefully to help you decide on the answer.

2. (a) Where does Mrs. Miller believe would be a good place to build a bike track?

   _____

   > **Think!**
   > You will need to read the beginning of paragraph 5 to find the answer.

   (b) Briefly explain why she believes this.

   _____

   _____

   _____

   _____

   > **Think!**
   > Underline keywords in paragraph 5 to help you find the details.

3. Explain why Mrs. Miller says riding down steep streets is dangerous.

   _____

   _____

   _____

   > **Think!**
   > Read paragraph 2 to find the answer.

4. Explain your point of view about bike tracks.

   _____

   _____

   _____

   > **Think!**
   > Think about what you know about bike tracks and what you read in the letter.

Name _____

Use the strategies you have been practicing to help you identify the writer's point of view.

1. Read the sentences about the area Mrs. Miller thinks would be good for a bike track. Which would she **not** agree with?

    (a)   Younger children could play on the playground equipment.

    (b)   Parents and children would meet new people.

    (c)   Only children should go to the track.

    (d)   The grassy area would be a good place to sit.

2. Explain why Mrs. Miller believes that driveways are not suitable places to ride.

    _____

    _____

    _____

    _____

3. What is Mrs. Miller's point of view about paying for the bike track?

    _____

    _____

    _____

    _____

4. Mrs. Miller's purpose in writing the letter was to persuade the city council to build a bike track. How well do you think she did this?

    (a)   very well

    (b)   well

    (c)   not well

    (d)   not at all

Name _____

Activity: Read the poem below and complete page 108.

Double Trouble

1.   I have twin baby brothers
They are eighteen months old
Together they sure are a handful
But they'll get better—so I'm told!

2.   Their names are Trent and Brent
My parents like the way they rhyme
But isn't it confusing?
I get them muddled all the time!

3.   Both have round, chubby faces
Blond hair and eyes of blue
Thank goodness Trent's hair is slightly curly
Or I'd never know who's who!

4.   They wake up bright and early
And want some milk to drink
Then I help Mom change their diapers
And boy—they sure do stink!

5.   The family room is always messy
Filled with crumbs, wet clothes, and toys
Two bouncers, a double stroller, and a play pen
A lot of stuff for two small boys!

6.   My brothers are double trouble
But we don't really mind
Because having two, not one
Means double love, we find!

Try It Out

Name _____

Use the strategies you learned and practiced in *Request for a Bike Track* to help you identify the writer's point of view and purpose.

Remember:

- Writers don't always just tell you what they think or believe or why they have written the text. Sometimes, you have to try to think like they do and form a conclusion based on the information you have read.
- In the text, there are details and information for you to find to help you choose the correct answer to each question. This information could be underlined.
- Consider all possible answers before making a decision.

1. What was the writer's main reason for writing the poem?
    (a)   To tell the reader he or she has twin brothers.
    (b)   To make the reader laugh.
    (c)   To tell the reader what it is like living with twin brothers.
    (d)   To tell the reader the names of his or her twin brothers.

Think!
Read each answer carefully and think about the one that explains the reason the best.

2. Explain what the writer thinks about his or her parents' choice of names for the twins.

    _____

    _____

3. Which of these would the writer *not* agree with?
    (a)   The twins have smelly diapers.
    (b)   The twins are easy to look after.
    (c)   The twins make a lot of messes.
    (d)   The twins are hard to tell apart.

4. The writer says his or her twin brothers are double trouble. Do you think he or she really believes this is true?

    Yes ◯   No ◯

    Explain why you chose this answer.

    _____

    _____

Name _____

Activity: Read the story below, and use pages 110–112 to show how well you can recognize cause and effect, fact or opinion, and the writer's point of view and purpose.

Flight to Singapore

1.   Last year, our family spent a week in Singapore. To travel there, we had a ten-hour flight on a jumbo jet. That's a long, long time!

2.   Before we left, Mom helped my younger sister and me pack our backpacks with things to do on the flight. We put in notebooks, puzzles, reading and coloring books, and pencils. We also packed our music player with our favorite songs downloaded.

3.   The taxi ride to the airport took 45 minutes, which seemed like ages. Dad said that was nothing compared to how long the rest of the trip would take! Finally, we boarded the plane. My sister and I sat in the seats in front of Mom and Dad.

4.   As we took off, Mom gave us some gum to chew. She said it would make our ears go "pop" and stop them from aching, which sometimes happens when you are taking off or landing.

5.   Next, the flight attendant carefully explained what to do in the event of an emergency. He showed us how to put on the life jacket hidden under the seat, how to attach the mask that drops down if more oxygen is needed in the plane, and how to get out of the plane by following lights on the floor.

6.   After a while, we were brought meals that we ate on trays we pulled down from the seats in front of us. It was great fun—like having a picnic! The only bad thing was that I wanted to go to the bathroom, but my sister hadn't finished her meal, and I had to climb under her tray to get past.

7.   The flight attendant very kindly showed us how to get the TV screen out of the armrest where it was folded up. It was a bit tricky. The movie that they showed us was suitable for adults and kids. We'd seen it before and had enjoyed it. It took two hours to watch, so it made some of the time pass.

8.   We spent the next few hours doing things we had brought in our backpacks. My sister started being a pain and kept asking how much longer before we got to Singapore. For me, the time passed much quicker than I thought it would. This is probably because I slept for a while and my sister didn't. We looked out the window as we got closer to the ground, ready to land. Singapore was full of tall buildings and heaps of apartment blocks— as there are so many people living on the island.

9.   It was good to get out of the plane and stretch our legs. Now all we had to do was collect our luggage, and the next part of our vacation would begin!

Assessment

Name _____

> **Remember:**
>
> - A cause leads to an effect, and they are connected.
> - You will be told one, and you will need to identify the other.
> - Look for keywords in the question and underline them.
> - Find words in the text that are connected to keywords in the question.
> - Check all answers before deciding.

1. What effect does chewing gum during take-off have?
   (a) It makes your ears ache.
   (b) It passes the time.
   (c) The gum tastes nice.
   (d) It makes your ears "pop."

2. What is the cause of a mask dropping down in a plane?

   _____

   _____

3. How did Mom try to prevent the kids from being bored on the flight?

   _____

   _____

   _____

4. What caused the writer to feel as if the time on the flight passed quickly?
   (a) The writer slept during the whole flight.
   (b) The writer ate, watched a movie, read, and slept on the flight.
   (c) The writer watched three movies and slept on the flight.
   (d) The writer listened to music, did puzzles, and played video games on the flight.

Fact or Opinion

Name _____

> **Remember:**
> - A fact can be checked and proven to be correct.
> - An opinion is what someone *believes* to be true, but it can't be proven.
> - Always check all possible answers before making a decision.

1. Which sentence is a fact?

(a)   The kids flew in a jumbo jet.

(b)   The flight took a very long time.

(c)   The movie was great.

(d)   The kids thought the food was delicious.

2. Which sentence is an opinion?

(a)   The family spent a week in Singapore.

(b)   The flight took ten hours.

(c)   The life jacket was hidden under the seat.

(d)   The meal on the plane was like having a picnic.

3. Read this sentence from the text and write a sentence with one fact and a sentence with one opinion.

The taxi ride to the airport took 45 minutes, which seemed like ages.

Fact: _____

_____

Opinion: _____

_____

4. What was Dad's opinion of the trip to the airport by taxi?

_____

_____

_____

> **Remember:**
> - Writers don't always tell you what they think or believe or why they have written the text. Sometimes, you have to try to think like they do and form a conclusion based on what you have read.
> - In the text, there are details and information for you to find to help you choose the correct answer to each question. This information could be underlined.
> - Consider all possible answers before making a decision.

1. What was the writer's main reason for writing the text?
   (a) To tell the reader about Singapore.
   (b) To make the reader laugh.
   (c) To tell the reader what it is like on a plane trip.
   (d) To explain what a flight attendant does on a plane.

2. Which of these would the writer *not* agree with?
   (a) The flight attendant was kind.
   (b) The writer's sister was patient the whole time.
   (c) The flight attendant explained things well.
   (d) It can be difficult to get to the bathroom on plane.

3. Explain what you think the writer thought of flight attendants.

   _____

   _____

4. What was the writer's point of view about the flight overall?

   _____

   _____

   _____

   _____